Friends
Helping
Friends:

A Handbook for Helpers

Second Edition

by
Carol Painter

Friends Helping Friends: A Handbook for Helpers
—*Second Edition*

Copyright ©2003

Educational Media Corporation®
P.O. Box 21311
Minneapolis, MN 55421-0311

(763) 781-0088 or (800) 966-3382

http://www.**educationalmedia**.com

Library of Congress Catalog Card No. 2002113188
ISBN 1-930572-21-2
Printing (Last Digit)
10   9   8   7   6   5   4   3   2   1

Production editor—
Don L. Sorenson

Graphic design—
Earl Sorenson

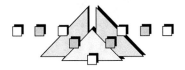

To all the peer helpers I have known and loved—

May God give you the grace to be the friend

you would like to have.

Table of Contents

An Open Letter

Dear Peer Helper:

In opening this book you have just taken the first step in a journey that will change your life and the lives of others. You have the opportunity to provide a service that no one else can accomplish in quite the same way. The priceless gift you offer is the gift of *yourself.*

You'll be learning to be a better friend. You'll be a friend to people who would not have met you otherwise. You'll be a friend to people who are different from you. Yet, in all the people you meet, the thing they'll have in common is their need for a special friend. They need—as we all do—a friend to help them recognize their worth, their strengths, their solutions in life. They need someone to help them see that life is worth living, worth treasuring, even when it hurts.

To do this important job requires some special training. Part of the training will be an opportunity for you to deal with your own painful feelings. To be effective helpers, you have to deal with your own feelings first. Unless you are growing, you can't help others to grow.

Another part of the training involves learning the skills of helping. There are identifiable skills that every effective helper possesses. You may find that you already have some of these skills. This is because some people are "natural helpers." Yet, a sad thing happens in every training group. Some of the people who have a natural gift for helping simply rely upon it rather than using it to develop further. Because they don't stretch, they stagnate. Don't let this be you. Become totally involved in the training experience.

A third part of the training involves topics such as suicide, alcoholism, grief, divorce, and others. This gives you the background you will need to respond effectively. You also will learn when to make referrals to a professional because some situations will call for more expertise than you possess. You'll meet many professionals from your school and community, and these people will be part of your helping network.

You're going to learn many, many new things. Perhaps the greatest thing you'll learn is how to be a friend *to yourself*. This is actually one of the hardest lessons most of us have to learn. However, when we finally learn how to be our own best friend, the world becomes a more positive place. Then we begin to understand that there are no real failures. There are only lessons. So every time you face a challenge, remember that you are capable of learning and beginning anew. Life will look very different.

My love and respect,

Carol Painter

Section I
Helper Development

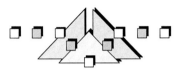

Chapter 1

Pitfalls on the Path

We need to have a philosophy of helping and to understand the pitfalls of helping to be effective helpers. Here are some issues for you to consider:

Being a Friend *to Yourself*

We need balance in our lives to be effective. We need to be having positive experiences ourselves in order to have extra energy and love to give others. However, this can't happen if we criticize everything we do, say, and feel. Yet, this is exactly the pitfall into which many of us step.

Consider for a moment what a relationship like this would be like. If we wanted to see our friends improve, we'd remind them constantly of past failures and of the ways they're inadequate. If someone pointed out their good qualities, we'd say, *"Sometimes maybe, but usually they just don't live up to my expectations."*

Whoa, partner. It's hard to picture a friendship based on this kind of interaction, isn't it? Then why do you suppose this describes the way many of us treat ourselves? What we would never do to other people is exactly what we do to ourselves, and it doesn't serve us any more than it would help them.

Most of us are out of balance in this way. We can tell you all our faults instantly, yet watch how long it takes to list the things we do well. It's true that we need to look at the ways we can improve. However, if this isn't balanced by our positive qualities, we'll succeed only in making it seem like a hopeless struggle. We all grow best in an atmosphere of acceptance and love, including the atmosphere we create for ourselves. Personal growth needs to be seen as the exciting process it is, not as punishment we inflict on ourselves. What we hope to give to our friends must begin with us.

Selfishness

This is a common helper issue and one of the most difficult. The feeling is that we must be ready to give people what they need, when they need it, for whatever time they need it. This is sometimes possible for short periods of time, such as in crisis situations.

However, most of the time this is neither realistic nor healthy. There is a significant difference between *selfishness* and *self-centeredness*. There is a difference between being responsible *to* people and being responsible *for* people. We must learn what we're responsible for *and* what others are responsible for. When we do for others what they need to be doing for themselves, we actually weaken them. We must set healthy limits or boundaries in our relationships. Within the safety of these boundaries, we are free to help—to support and encourage—people without taking up their burdens as our own.

We are responsible for ourselves physically, emotionally, and spiritually. If we try to stay constantly in the *role* of helper, we'll become dangerously overextended. Ironically, t h e n we'll end up withdrawing from the person, causing the very pain we were trying to prevent in the first place. The pitfall here is in knowing when we must say no. We can't give more than we have. If we don't save enough of ourselves *for ourselves*, we'll have nothing to give others.

And, if we ever help others because we think we *should*, people sense it. They come away feeling inferior and burdensome. This kind of "helping" may create more resentment than respect between people.

Our nature is selfish. We do the things we do because we get something out of doing them. Helping is no exception. We have all chosen to be helpers because we help ourselves every time we help someone else. Giving becomes receiving.

Responsibility

This is not a word that young people like to hear very often, probably because they *do* hear it so often. However, the concept of responsibility is one of the most empowering—and misunderstood—ideas that exist. Most of us think of responsibility as having to do things we don't want to do. However, responsibility is actually power, and understanding this will change our life.

When we recognize that we have responsibility in an area, it follows that we also have control and can affect change. By changing *our* actions, we change the way others respond to us. We are proactive rather than reactive. We move from a victim or blaming stance into accepting responsibility for the changes we would like to see.

We tend to resist responsibility for our feelings, relationships, and decisions. Sometimes we go so far as wanting others to decide for us, believing it's easier. Our unconscious thinking is: *"If I make a decision but don't like the way it turns out, I'll have only myself to blame. But if I let other people decide, then I can blame them if things don't turn out the way I want."*

There is no harder way to live. Very few of us like decisions made for us because it's not what we would have done. Taking responsibility frees us to change our life.

Feelings

Encouraging others to be aware of and honest about their feelings is essential. Helpers often are afraid at first that focusing on feelings will make people feel worse, especially when the feelings are painful.

Yet, we do no service in helping people hide from their feelings. When feelings seem overwhelming or situations seem hopeless, people often say, *"Just forget it."* This is intended to be helpful, but it avoids what the person is experiencing. The one saying this is caught in the trap of believing that people are victims of their feelings.

But we choose our feelings. You cannot *make* me angry. If I'm angry, it's because I *choose* to be angry. How else can you explain that things make some people angry but not others? Our feelings are caused by our thoughts. It's not what happens to us, but what we *think* about what happens to us that determines how we feel.

For example, let's say that when you go to your locker, the guy next to you looks at you and says, *"Nerd!"* If you think he's right, you're going to be depressed. If you think instead that he must be having a really bad day to turn his anger on you for no reason, you might *feel* sorry for him. You could decide it doesn't have anything to do with you. You also could decide that he *needs a friend like you.*

We can change our *feelings* by changing our *thoughts.* By thinking differently we can feel differently. This is why there's always something we can do about any situation. We can always *choose* to feel differently.

Accepting the Faces People Wear

We all have basically the same feelings, fears, and needs. The difference is only a matter of degree. For example, we've all felt angry at some time. I may feel angry only occasionally, whereas you may feel angry frequently. Regardless, anger is an emotion we've both experienced. I may show my anger by withdrawing and being quiet, and you may show your anger by yelling and throwing things. If we let ourselves be separated by the different ways we respond, we'll miss the connection.

We also have different ways of dealing with the same fears and needs. One of the needs we have is to be accepted and liked. So one of our fears is that we won't be. Some people respond by becoming shy and introverted while others become braggarts. Braggarts give the *impression* of being supremely confident and self-satisfied. Yet, as is true with people so often, things are just the opposite of the way they seem. If we don't look closely, we'll miss the fact that both people have the same fear, but different ways of responding.

When we *accept people* no matter what face they wear, it sets up a gracious cycle in our lives. The more we accept and understand other people, the better we accept and understand ourselves. The gentler we are with ourselves, the more loving we are to others.

Seeing Problems as Problems

How we see problems determines the quality of our interventions. If we see problems as heavy loads people must carry in their lives, it affects our response. We'll feel pity for people and wonder why they're so unlucky. Unfortunately, when people sense this, it confirms their fears and reinforces their feelings of helplessness and self-pity.

However, when we see problems as opportunities, we transmit a completely different attitude. Life is change and challenge. If it were too easy, we wouldn't learn. If it never challenged us, we wouldn't grow.

Of course we all prefer the trouble-free periods of life. However, when we understand that our problems come in order to teach a lesson we need, it becomes a completely different experience. Then we put our energy into asking ourselves *what* we need to learn rather than asking ourselves *why* this had to happen.

The ironic part is that the more we accept our problems, the fewer we have. The pitfall for the helper is in forgetting that the tough times also are the times of greatest growth.

Excellence Without Practice

Those who strive to be Olympic downhill racers never would imagine that they could accomplish their dreams without a great deal of practice. Most contenders know that talent alone won't suffice without a great deal of trial and error, effort and dedication to go with it.

If you've ever learned to drive a car with a stick shift, you have a wonderful mental picture of the process we go through when we learn something new. There are the stop and go starts, the grinding gears, and the stalled engine in the middle of the busy intersection to show us that we need more practice.

Yet, have you ever noticed that people expect to become an expert in communication with only one try? Take, for example, the young woman who decides to be more assertive with her boyfriend. When he snaps at her instead of listening, however, she decides that assertiveness doesn't work. Or, what about the young man who decides to talk with his father about their interactions? When he ends up grounded for two months, he decides it's entirely too risky to tell anyone how he feels.

Our Olympic downhill racers undoubtedly came off the starting block many times believing that *this* was going to be the perfect run—and then landed flat on their faces. Somehow we accept this when we're trying to develop a physical skill. There's no shame, but rather a dedication to work all the harder the next day. However, when we want to develop an emotional or interpersonal skill, we often decide after one attempt that it can't be done. If we can't deliver a smooth and perfect result the first time, we quit. We give up the dream.

Advice Giving

The most common misconception of counseling is that it's advice giving. An essential part of what you'll learn is how to help others *without* telling them what to do. You'll learn instead to be a caring and effective *listener,* perhaps offering a different perspective and always facilitating *their* problem-solving process.

There are many pitfalls in giving advice. The first is that if we always solve problems for people, they never learn to do it for themselves. This means that every time they have a problem, guess who they're going to need to solve it for them? A second problem is that the advice we give can have disastrous consequences. Ask yourself this question: *"How responsible are you for the results of your advice?"* Scary thought. A third problem with giving advice is that we only know one side of the issue. Without knowing the whole story, we can actually encourage problem behaviors.

The ironic part about advice is that people often ask for it, but they rarely like it. Have you ever had people ask what they should do and when you answered, they said *"Yes, but..."* and gave several reasons why it wouldn't work? We call those ya-buts. If you're getting ya-buts from people, it's a signal that you're giving advice and they're resisting. Usually when people ask for advice, what they're *really* asking for is our time and attention, even if they don't quite say so.

However, there are times when a person *does* want to know what we would do. Be careful. The best way I can share *my* perspective on *your* situation is to tell you what I might do if I were in your shoes. Each of us must find our own answers.

Needing to Make the Right Decisions

It would be nice if all our decisions were right, meaning that we never regretted our choice. For some people however, the need to make the right decision becomes an obsession. Then making *any* decision becomes almost impossible. Rather than risk making the wrong decision, they simply float along waiting for people or events to make their decision for them.

The only way to make the right decision is to know—in advance—how it will turn out. We can make fairly accurate predictions as to what will happen if we do a certain thing. However, we simply cannot know the future. We gather all the available information, and then it comes down to a choice on our part. We make what appears to be the best decision, and then we work to make it right. We make it work or we use it as a learning process.

Once we understand that we won't always do the perfect thing at the right time, we accept where we are and move closer to where we want to be. Progress becomes a series of short zig-zag lines that point in the direction we're heading. The pitfall lies in believing that the only acceptable progress is that of a straight, unbroken line.

Trying

We can't try to do anything. We either do it, or we don't do it. You can't try to stand, for example. Go ahead. You'll find that you're either sitting or standing. What we think of as trying to stand is something we do while we're still sitting.

Take the word out of your vocabulary. Replace it instead with expressions that indicate whether you will or won't do something. For example, rather than saying, *"I'll try to call you tonight,"* say, *"I will make time to call tonight"* or *"I won't be calling tonight."*

Notice the shift in focus that occurs when we express ourselves this way. Rather than offering excuses, we remind ourselves that ultimately it's our choice. The words we use to communicate with others carry a great deal of power in determining our choices and need to be monitored with care.

Self-Talk

The words we use to communicate *with ourselves* also carry a great deal of power and need to be monitored with care. People often have extremely negative conversations in their heads. Sound strange? Test this by monitoring how many negative comments you make to yourself in a day.

The commentary sounds like this: *"Ugh! I look terrible this morning. Even worse than usual if that's possible... Oooh, I'm going to be late again. I never do anything right... Aagh, I've got my English test first thing this morning, and I know I'll fail. I'm so stupid. No wonder everyone avoids me. I would if I could...."*

This kind of self-talk becomes what is called *self-fulfilling prophecy.* That means we tend to make happen what we believe will happen. If we say—or someone else says—something long enough, we tend to believe it. For example, people who have been told all their lives that they're clumsy usually will begin to believe that they're clumsy, and they will become even clumsier.

Be Healthy

We now know that much illness is emotional in origin. Sometimes we make ourselves sick. Years ago I noticed that every time I became ill, it was on a Friday night. I thought it was quite a coincidence so I began to pay attention. I discovered that when I didn't feel well during the week, I would tell myself, *"I don't have time to be sick."* When Friday night came I unconsciously said, *"Now I can be sick."*

When I recognized what I was doing, I said, *"Hold everything! Maybe now I have time to be sick, but I don't want to be sick."* Since I had no time during the week and no interest on the weekend, the only solution was to stop altogether.

Since discovering this way of thinking, I have been ill only a few times. When I show symptoms, I say, *"I don't want to be sick."* I mean it when I say it, and I also decide how to take better care of myself.

Obviously this doesn't always work. However, we sometimes *participate* in our illness. We repeatedly tell ourselves, *"I'm getting sick."* Our bodies are designed for health, but our subconscious minds follow our directions even to the point of making us ill.

A helper requires a healthy lifestyle, physically and mentally. You'll be exposed to many new ideas and experiences during training. If you're gone, you'll have gaps in your learning. You'll miss experiences that can't be repeated. Consistency is essential. Be there.

Intuition

The most connected way of living occurs when people "follow their heart." We all have heard that small, still voice inside. My experience is that when I *listen*, I make the best decisions. When I ignore my heart's message, it's because I've gotten too hurried, or I've become stubborn and prideful, or I'm concerned about what other people will think. Inevitably I wish I had listened.

Others opt for the "logical" thing, meaning what the world says is best. They do this rather than doing what they know deep inside is right.

Intuition is our sensitive side through which ideas and feelings come into our awareness. Intellect is our active, problem-solving side. Using our intuition means learning to think with our mind but *decide* from our heart.

Intuition also plays a role in helping. You may find that intuition tells you more than a person's words are saying. If the thought occurs to you, then it needs to be explored with the person. To honor your intuition is to honor your heart.

Projection

It's interesting how we see others and the world. It's not at all unusual for two people to see the same person differently or to feel differently about the same event. Our feelings are *subjective* rather than *objective*. We see things as we are, rather than as they are.

People *project* their thoughts and feelings onto others. For example, a man who accuses his girlfriend of cheating often has cheated on her or has thought of cheating. Or, the girl who has been unjustly criticized by her parents may believe that others are being unjustly criticized. We often see in other people what *we* feel or think or do. We see their situation from *our* point of view, not theirs. The pitfall for the helper is in not dealing sufficiently with our own issues.

We also project our beliefs onto the world. If we believe that the world is made up of people who will like us, we'll be warm and outgoing. People will like us. However, if we believe that no one will like us, we'll be cold and aloof. And people will reject us. People react to our reactions.

Fear

Fear is at the root of most problems. It affects how we feel about ourselves, other people, and how we perceive life. For example, we're afraid to try out for a team because we'd feel like a failure if we didn't make it. Or, we're afraid to talk with an interesting group of people standing in the hallway because they might be offended. Or, we fear life because we're afraid of what could go wrong.

It's natural to want to run from our fears, but then they're always nipping at our heels. To face and express our fear is to control it. Otherwise we may create the very thing we fear.

Consider the girl who's afraid that her boyfriend doesn't really care. She's afraid that he's going to stop seeing her. So she worries about saying or doing the wrong thing. She's tense, and she swings from being argumentative to trying too hard to please. Her boyfriend has stronger feelings for her than for anyone he's ever known. But she's changed. She doesn't seem to feel the same. So he decides to stop seeing her. Out of fear she caused the very thing she was afraid would happen.

Or, consider the guy who hates speaking before a group. He imagines that people will laugh at him and think he's weird. So he's miserable and completely unlike himself. He turns sideways and won't even look up from his notes. He expresses himself strangely, mumbling a lot, and some of them decide that he's kind of weird. Out of fear he caused the very thing he was afraid would happen.

We also fear feelings. We're afraid that if we start, we won't be able to stop. We're afraid that we'll lose control and the feeling will take over. But it works in just the opposite way. The more we deny a feeling, the more likely it is to spill over at the worst possible moment.

We make a startling number of choices, and our choices are either fear choices or growth choices. Which will you choose?

Unconditional Love

Unconditional love isn't romantic love. Unconditional love doesn't even mean that we *like* a person. It doesn't mean we're blind to faults or mistakes. It doesn't mean we ignore our feelings and needs. It doesn't mean we stop making evaluations.

It *does* mean that our evaluations carry no judgment. Unconditional love means seeing people without judging them as good or bad. It means understanding that what they do is a result of what they know. Unconditional love means accepting *people*, not behavior.

We all enjoy being with people we like, but we learn the most from the people we don't like. People are our mirrors. Often what we see in them that we don't like is also true of us.

Being kind to those who are kind to us is easy. Liking the people who like us is the most natural thing in the world. The test of who we are comes when we're able to return rejection with acceptance and to replace conflict with compassion.

Unconditional love means learning to live generously and graciously. It's one of our greatest reasons for being.

Should-ing on Yourself

Many people live under the tyranny of *should*. If you recognize yourself in these examples, you may be should-ing on yourself—and others.

Example: You run for an office in school or in a club, and you're not elected.

Should-ing

"I should have gotten elected. Since people didn't vote for me, they obviously don't like me and don't think I'd do a good job."

Accepting

"I'm disappointed I didn't get elected. But I did meet a lot of new people and that was great."

Example: You've finally gotten a date with this great girl. You're having dinner at a nice restaurant. When you reach for your glass, you spill it all over the table and on your date.

Should-ing

"What a klutz! I should be more sophisticated. No way will she ever want to go out with me again."

Accepting

"I'm embarrassed. I guess I'm more nervous than I realized. I've looked forward to this for so long that I'm putting too much pressure on myself."

Example: You volunteered to work with a student who is having trouble at home and has asked to talk with a peer helper. However, it's becoming obvious that he or she isn't comfortable with you.

Should-ing

"I should be able to talk to anyone since I'm a peer helper. This just shows I'm not going to be any good at this. I'd better stick to working with people I know."

Accepting

"I'm sorry this isn't working out. I would have liked to help. I know how hard it is to open up, though. I'll just make sure he knows I care and that I'll be around."

Example: You and your parents are fighting lately. You know deep down that you're a big part of the problem, but they've done a lot to make things worse, too.

Should-ing

"You should be able to make things work around here without my help. You're the parents. It's one thing for me to make mistakes, but you should know better!"

Accepting

"This must be hard for everyone since no one is handling it well. I can see some things I could do to help. Maybe I'm the one to change."

When you *should* on yourself (or others), you punish yourself (or others) for the fact that you (or they) are not perfect. When you accept yourself (or others), you allow life experiences to be lessons for growth.

Section II
Skill Development

Chapter 2

Attending Skill

Attending is the first and most fundamental skill of peer helping. Because attending skills are easy to master, it's also easy to assume they're not as important as some of the more difficult skills we'll learn. However, all of the other skills are based upon an almost automatic ability to attend to a person in a helping relationship. Although attending looks and sounds easy, it requires a high level of energy and concentration.

Think how often you hear people say, *"You're not even listening to me!"* Usually what's happened is the listener is glancing around, or looking through a magazine, or staring into space. Even though this person may have heard every word, the non-attending behavior has communicated a lack of involvement. It's not enough to listen to people. We also must *look* like we're listening to them.

Ivey and Hinkle (1970) showed an interesting example of the power of attending. Six students in a psychology class planned an experiment on attending, using their professor as the target. They started class slouched in their chairs, listening only passively. At a prearranged signal, the students switched to attentive postures using active eye contact with the professor. When *they* changed, he changed from a monotone to animated gestures and facial expressions. A lively discussion followed. At another prearranged signal, the students reverted back to slouching and passive listening. After several futile attempts, the poor professor slipped back into his monotone and class ended on that note.

Attending utilizes specific behaviors. Most of these involve body postures that communicate availability. Facing the other person squarely is the posture that most clearly shows involvement. An "open" posture demonstrates respect and shows that the helper is open to what the person has to say. Crossed arms and legs sometimes signal when people are "closed" to a person or are in disagreement. Leaning toward the person is a sign of presence and involvement, while leaning away often signals withdrawal or resistance.

Eye contact is another important attending behavior. It involves looking comfortably at people without intruding upon them by staring. Looking at people is a way of demonstrating involvement, but it's also an essential tool for gathering information. Body language often reflects feelings more accurately than the words people use. A great deal of information and understanding will be lost if we don't look at people when they talk. Attending means listening not only with our ears but with our eyes and also our heart.

An effective helper also is relatively relaxed. It's terribly difficult to listen well when we're nervous. We have a tendency to interrupt or to jump in too quickly. We may even miss what a person is saying because we're so worried about how we're going to respond. Our nervousness eventually makes the people we're with nervous as well. Learn to forget yourself and to focus completely on the other person. Concern yourself only with how the other person is feeling. You'll find your nervousness disappears.

A helper also uses what are called "minimal encourages to talk." These include nodding the head, saying um-hmm, and repeating one or two words or asking short questions. These allow people to continue talking, without our jumping in prematurely with solutions.

As you become more aware of your attending behaviors, what may happen next is that you catch yourself one day with your arms crossed, leaning away from someone. Being aware of your physical posture makes you more aware of your emotional posture. Attending is the first step in becoming more effective friends.

Please Hear What I'm Not Saying

Don't be fooled by me.
Don't be fooled by the face I wear,
    for I wear a mask. I wear a thousand masks.
Masks that I'm afraid to take off,
    but none of them are me.
Pretending is an art that's second nature to me,
    but don't be fooled.
I give the impression that I'm secure,
    that all is sunny and unruffled with me,
    within as well as without.
That confidence is my name and coolness my game,
    and that I need no one.
Don't believe me.
Please.
My surface may be smooth, but my surface is my mask,
    my ever-concealing mask.
Beneath dwells the real me,
    in confusion and fear, in loneliness.
I idly talk in the smooth tones of surface chatter.
I tell you everything that's nothing
    of what's crying within me.
So when I'm going through my routine,
    please don't be fooled.
Please listen carefully,
    and try to hear what I'm not saying,
    but would like to say.
Each time you're kind, and gentle, and encouraging,
    my heart begins to grow wings,
    very small, feeble wings,
    but wings.

With your sympathy and sensitivity,
    you encourage me.
I want you to know how important you are,
    how you can be a part of the person that is me
    if you choose to.
Please choose to.
Don't pass me by.
It won't be easy for you.
My sense of worthlessness builds strong walls.
The nearer you approach,
    the blinder I may strike back.
I fight against the very thing I cry out for,
    but I am told that love is stronger than walls.
This is my only hope.
Who am I, you wonder?
    I'm someone you know well.
    I'm a member of your family.
    I'm the person sitting beside you.
    I'm a person you meet on the street.
Please don't believe my mask.
Please speak to me,
    share some of yourself with me.
At least recognize me.
Please.

Author Unknown
Condensed and Revised

Skills Chart

Make a check mark in a box next to a behavior each time the behavior is demonstrated:

I. Attending Skill

Sits facing the person ❑ ❑ ❑ ❑ ❑

Maintains good eye contact ❑ ❑ ❑ ❑ ❑

Maintains open, available posture ❑ ❑ ❑ ❑ ❑

Appears relaxed ❑ ❑ ❑ ❑ ❑

Gives encouragement, such as nodding head ❑ ❑ ❑ ❑ ❑

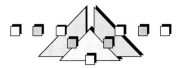

Chapter 3
Empathy Skill

Empathy is the second skill of peer helping. Empathy is the single most identifiable skill in effective helpers, no matter what their style, training, or personality. This skill comes from deep within and is what contributes most to the healing relationship that develops.

Empathy is often confused with *sympathy*. Sympathy tends to reinforce weakness rather than challenge growth. Sympathy often reflects a belief that there's nothing a person can do. It usually sounds something like, *"Poor baby."*

Empathy is the ability to understand a person's feelings as if they were our own—while remembering that they're *not* our own. Empathy is being able to feel from another person's perspective. An empathic helper responds with compassion and acceptance, but also with respect and a belief that the person will cope.

Empathic responses reflect back the *essence* of what people say but in our own words. When we accept and mirror people's thoughts and feelings, we show that they're not so different from us. One of the fears people have when things go wrong is that there must be something *wrong with them*. When we can empathize, it allows them to move away from this fear into a clearer understanding and perspective.

Empathic responses also allow a helper to respond frequently to people without taking the focus away from them. They give a helper time to gather more information and to come to a deeper understanding. They guard against the impulse to jump in prematurely with a solution while a person still has feelings and thoughts left unsaid or unexplored. Empathic responses guard the helper from jumping in with, *"What you should do is...."*

Here are some examples of empathic responses:

Friend:

"I think I just failed my history test. My boss told me last night that he's not satisfied with my work. And now I see my girlfriend talking to that guy again!"

Helper:

"Sometimes it seems like everything goes wrong at once.

Friend:

"I should be making decisions about next year, but I don't know what to do. I just keep putting it off."

Helper:

"It's nerve-racking when you need to be doing something, but you don't know what to do."

Friend:

"My boyfriend is spending a lot of time with his old girlfriend again. When I asked him about it, he said there wasn't anything to it. But he wouldn't tell me what they talked about either."

Helper:

"It's hard to trust him when he won't help you understand what's going on."

Empathy develops trust and openness between people, and the understanding it reflects leads to deeper and more honest responses. People become *free* to know their feelings and to recognize their responses within a situation.

Becoming an Active Listener

It has been said that the reason we have two ears and only one mouth is because we're intended to spend twice as much time listening as talking. People are naturally drawn to good listeners because they always feel better after being with them.

Active listening is a powerful tool for change and growth. Active listeners never just passively hear the words spoken. Instead they work to understand, accept, absorb, and respond to both the meaning and the feelings of the person speaking. This requires respect for the worth of people and an ability to suspend judgment, not having "walked a mile in their moccasins."

Active listening has no place for mental behaviors such as judging or analyzing why people do something or mentally arguing with them. These thoughts close the mind and interfere with the listener's ability to hear what is actually said.

Active listening conveys to people that we can see their point of view. We reach for the total meaning of what is said, listening for feelings *and* content. We stay focused on the main points and listen for relevant themes. We listen to what is said and what is not said, while noting *how* it is said.

Something very special happens when people are listened to in this way. They begin to listen *to themselves* more deeply. They explore their thoughts and feelings in new ways—and with new insights.

Listen

When I ask you to listen to me
    and you start giving advice,
    you haven't done what I ask.

When I ask you to listen to me
    and you begin to tell me
    why I shouldn't feel that way,
    you're trampling my feelings.

When I ask you to listen to me
    and you think you have to do something
    to solve my problems,
    you have failed me
    strange as that may seem.

Listen.

All I asked was that you listen,
    not talk or do, just hear me.

I can do for myself.

I'm not helpless,
    maybe discouraged and faltering,
    but not helpless.

When you do something for me
    that I need to do for myself,
    you contribute to my fear and weakness.

But when you accept as a simple fact
    that I feel what I feel,
    no matter how irrational,
    I quit trying to convince you
    and can begin to understand
    what's behind this irrational feeling.

And when that's clear,
    the answers are obvious and I don't need advice.

Irrational feelings make sense
    when we understand what's behind them.

So please listen and just hear me,
    and if you want to talk,
    wait just a bit
    and I'll listen to you.

Author Unknown, Revised

Reflection of Feelings and Content

Empathic helpers need an extensive feeling vocabulary to move out of "glad, mad, sad, bad" types of responses and into those which show more depth and definition.

Feelings: Levels of Intensity

Happy
(Strong) Ecstatic, Overjoyed, Thrilled

(Medium) Delighted, Gratified, Excited

(Mild) Pleased, Satisfied, Content

Angry
(Strong) Furious, Outraged, Seething

(Medium) Resentful, Exasperated, Irritated

(Mild) Upset, Annoyed, Ticked

Sad
(Strong) Miserable, Crushed, Heartbroken

(Medium) Depressed, Sorrowful, Dejected

(Mild) Down, Glum, Discouraged

Scared
(Strong) Terrified, Horrified, Alarmed

(Medium) Intimidated, Anxious, Startled

(Mild) Nervous, Uneasy, Unsettled

Confused
(Strong) Bewildered, Disconcerted, Overwhelmed

(Medium) Doubtful, Unsure, Mixed Up

(Mild) Vague, Puzzled, Undecided

Part I

Imagine listening to the people quoted here. Write a response that communicates empathy for their feelings. Select from the list or choose your own. Notice that different responses will occur to you depending on how you imagine the tone of voice.

Example

Friend:

"My best friends are fighting again, and they keep trying to get me to take sides."

Helper:

"You feel irritated."

1. **Friend:**

   "My parents don't trust me anymore."

   Helper:

   You feel _____ .

2. **Friend:**

   "Some days my friends act like I'm not even there.

   Helper:

   You feel _____ .

3. **Friend:**

   "I finally did it! I made the honor roll."

   Helper:

   You feel _____ .

4. **Friend:**

   "My girlfriend just broke up with me."

   Helper:

   You feel _____ .

5. **Friend:**

   "When my dad finds out I've been ditching class, he's going to be furious."

   Helper:

   You feel _____ .

Part II

Now we'll take the process one step further. The most complete response reflects both feelings *and* content. It demonstrates to people that we understand their feelings *and* their reasons. Imagine listening to the people quoted here. Write a response that communicates empathy for *both* feelings and content.

Example

Friend:

"I don't know if I should talk about it. My family says that what happens at home is private."

Helper:

"You feel confused about talking because of what your family says."

1. **Friend:**

   "I thought he was going to kick me out of class for sure. Instead he called me into his office, and we talked."

   Helper:

   You feel _____ *because* _____ .

2. **Friend:**

   "I can't quite figure him out. I can't tell if he really cares about me or is just using me to make Sherri jealous."

   Helper:

   You feel _____ *because* _____ .

3. **Friend:**

   "Everybody makes fun of my clothes. My family can't afford anything new. People don't have to like me, but I wish they'd stop making fun of me."

   Helper:

   You feel _____ *because* _____ .

4. Friend:

"I have a report due, and I have to work late tonight. The house is a mess, and my parents are coming home tomorrow."

Helper:

You feel _____ because _____ .

5. Friend:

"I had the best practices this week. Coach kept telling me what a good job I was doing, but I just found out I'm not starting in the game tomorrow."

Helper:

You feel _____ because _____ .

Part III

This is the last step in learning to reflect feelings and content. We'll focus now on more natural ways of responding. This time write your responses in your *own language and style*. Be sure you continue to reflect both feelings and content.

Example

Friend:

"I don't know if I should talk about it. My family says that what happens at home is private."

Helper:

"It can be confusing when you want to talk about something, but you're not sure it's okay."

1. **Friend:**

   "I thought he was going to kick me out of class for sure. Instead he called me into his office, and we talked."

   Helper:

2. **Friend:**

   "I can't quite figure him out. I can't tell if he really cares about me or is just using me to make Sherri jealous."

   Helper:

3. **Friend:**

   "Everybody makes fun of my clothes. My family can't afford anything new. People don't have to like me, but I wish they'd stop making fun of me."

   Helper:

4. **Friend:**

"*I have a report due, and I have to work late tonight. The house is a mess, and my parents are coming home tomorrow.*"

Helper:

5. **Friend:**

"*I had the best practices this week. Coach kept telling me what a good job I was doing, but I just found out I'm not starting in the game tomorrow.*"

Helper:

A Student's Saga

Imagine that you're at registration with a large group of students who are either waiting to change their schedule or to select their classes. People are sitting in chairs, on benches, and on the floor. The line is moving very slowly. Most of the students are laughing, talking, and enjoying seeing their friends again. However, the person sitting next to you is clearly upset. When he or she turns to you and starts talking, you decide to use your new empathy skills:

"Man, this stinks!"

Empathy response:

"These people act like we've got all day to sit here."

Empathy response:

"I didn't want to move here in the first place."

Empathy response:

"People aren't very friendly here. The kids look like they'd never notice someone new."

Empathy response:

"My friends back home are probably doing something together right now."

Empathy response:

"This never would have happened if my parents could just get along."

Empathy response:

"They don't know how to do anything but fight."

Empathy response:

"And that was bad enough, but then they said I had to move here with my mom."

Empathy response:

"I'm graduating this year. I don't know why I couldn't decide for myself where I would live."

Empathy response:

"They say this is a good school and things will be better for me here. How do they know?"

Empathy response:

"I have to admit I'll get into a better college from this school... and sometimes my dad drinks too much."

Empathy response:

"I know my mom's been worried about me lately, but I haven't wanted to talk to her."

Empathy response:

"I think I've made things harder for both of us."

Empathy response:

"I'll talk with her about it tonight."

Empathy response:

"I'm going to like this place if everyone is as understanding as you. Would you introduce me to some of your friends?"

An Exercise in Self-Disclosure

As a helper you'll be encouraging people to be open about their feelings and life experiences. We must never ask others to do what we're unwilling to do, and we *all* have areas to improve.

Your training is an opportunity to know and be known by a group of caring people. For that to happen you must be open. Your work in training triads is a perfect time for this. Instead of using role-play topics when you take the *role of friend*, you can talk about issues in *your* life. Besides the support you'll receive, you'll also learn what it feels like to receive help.

This exercise allows you to identify *in advance* the feelings and experiences you will discuss. Some examples of possible topics are listed. These are given only to stimulate your thinking.

Examples

"It's hard for me to meet new people and be open."

"My brother and I fight constantly."

"I'm too critical of myself."

"The only time I feel good is when I'm helping someone."

"My parents are getting a divorce."

Training Triad Topics:

1.

2.

3.

4.

5.

Skills Chart

Make a check mark in a box next to a behavior each time the behavior is demonstrated:

I. Attending Skill

Sits facing the person ❏ ❏ ❏ ❏ ❏

Maintains good eye contact ❏ ❏ ❏ ❏ ❏

Maintains open, available posture ❏ ❏ ❏ ❏ ❏

Appears relaxed ❏ ❏ ❏ ❏ ❏

Gives encouragement, such as nodding head ❏ ❏ ❏ ❏ ❏

II. Empathy Skill

Reflects feelings ❏ ❏ ❏ ❏ ❏

Reflects content ❏ ❏ ❏ ❏ ❏

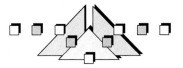

Chapter 4

Clarifying /Questioning Skill

The third skill of peer helping is that of *clarifying/questioning*. This skill is one that many people believe they've mastered because they use it so often. However, the skill of clarifying/questioning is both the most frequently used and the most frequently misused of all the skills we'll discuss.

Clarifying questions or statements are a natural part of a conversation. When we aren't sure we understand, we ask clarifying questions or make clarifying statements. For example:

"Are you saying that...?"

"So what you're saying is...."

"Do you mean...?"

However, clarifying questions or statements can serve other purposes as well. One is that they signal a person that we're actively following the conversation and want to understand. Clarifying questions or statements also can be used to highlight important thoughts and feelings being expressed. This sometimes encourages people to pause and think more deeply.

Effective questioning is a rare skill. Questioning can allow a person to open and a relationship to grow, or it can cause a person to withdraw and a relationship to close. The problem with questions is that we ask too many of them, and then we don't listen to the answers. Soon people feel like they're part of an interrogation rather than a dialogue.

Questions often are statements in disguise. If I say, *"You didn't like what he said, did you?"* I already have decided what the answer is. Instead I could say, *"If he had said that to me, I would be hurt. How do you feel?"* Or, if I say, *"Are you angry?"* and you're feeling tired, you have to explain or possibly defend yourself. I might have begun more effectively by observing, *"You seem quiet today."*

We need to consider which kind of question is most appropriate. There are two kinds. The *open* question allows people to express themselves in their own way, often providing unexpected information. The *closed* question has only the expectation of a yes or no answer and consequently gains little information.

Open questions offer an invitation and opportunity to talk. They typically begin with words such as *what, where, when, how,* or *who:*

"What would you like to do about this?"

"Where would you like to be in ten years?"

"When do you plan to begin?"

"How are you feeling?"

"Who has influenced you the most?"

Although questions that begin with *why* can be considered open, they need to be used sparingly. Questions such as *"Why did you do that?"* tend to make people defensive. People often don't realize why they did something until they've had a chance to sort through their feelings. Of course it's often the *way* a person is asked that determines the outcome. Why questions often can be replaced with *what* questions. I could ask, *"What were you feeling when you did that?"* or *"What were you hoping would happen?"*

Closed questions have a purpose, of course, when factual information is needed. They typically begin with words such as *is, are, do,* or *did:*

"Is it my turn?"

"Are you going to work today?"

"Do you mind if I have another piece of pie?"

"Did you call the doctor?"

Sometimes a closed question will be met with a full and complete answer if the person is outgoing or feels like talking. On the other hand an open question can be met with a short, incomplete answer if the person doesn't want to talk. The best example of this is the question, *"How was your day?"* Answer: *"Fine."*

Even so my best chance of initiating a meaningful conversation with you happens when I use the right questions.

Closed:

"Did you like school today?"

Open:

"What was the funniest thing that happened to you today?"

Closed:

"Are you embarrassed?"

Open:

"How do you feel?"

Closed:

"Is this the way you want things to be with us?"

Open:

"What kind of relationship do you want for us?"

Some Clarifying Questions

Try one of these in your next conversation:

1. How important is that to you?
2. What is another choice you have?
3. How did you feel when that happened?
4. What did you do when he (or she) did that?
5. Are you glad about that?
6. What are your reasons for saying that?
7. Was that your choice?
8. What would you like to have happen?
9. Can you give me an example?
10. What would happen if you did that?
11. Can you tell me what you mean by that?
12. What is your next step?
13. Would you do it the same way again?
14. What are some good things about that?
15. Can you do anything about that?
16. What would need to happen for it to work out that way?
17. How long have you felt this way?
18. What makes that difficult for you?
19. Is that what you believe or what you know?
20. What is the most painful part for you?
21. What would you say if you had the chance?
22. What matters the most to you about that?
23. What do you need to know?
24. What would it take for you to feel differently?
25. What would your best friend tell you to do?

Skills Chart

Make a check mark in a box next to a behavior each time the behavior is demonstrated:

I. Attending Skill

Sits facing the person ❑ ❑ ❑ ❑ ❑

Maintains good eye contact ❑ ❑ ❑ ❑ ❑

Maintains open, available posture ❑ ❑ ❑ ❑ ❑

Appears relaxed ❑ ❑ ❑ ❑ ❑

Gives encouragement, such as nodding head ❑ ❑ ❑ ❑ ❑

II. Empathy Skill

Reflects feelings ❑ ❑ ❑ ❑ ❑

Reflects content ❑ ❑ ❑ ❑ ❑

III. Clarifying/Questioning Skill

Uses clarifying questions or statements ❑ ❑ ❑ ❑ ❑

Asks open questions ❑ ❑ ❑ ❑ ❑

Asks closed questions ❑ ❑ ❑ ❑ ❑

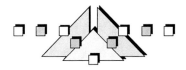

Chapter 5

Assertiveness Skill

The fourth skill of peer helping is *assertiveness*. Assertiveness is an unusual skill in that people perceive it differently. When females think of an assertive woman, they may imagine a pushy, bristly person. When males think of an assertive man, they may picture a weak, whining person. This comes largely from the way we're conditioned, depending upon our gender. Females are conditioned to be pleasing, giving, and pacifying. Males are conditioned to be strong and aggressive, doing what is necessary to achieve their goals.

In a very broad and general sense, male and female behaviors represent opposite ends of a behavior spectrum. The conditioned female response can be seen as representing the passive end of the spectrum, and the conditioned male response can be seen as representing the aggressive end of the spectrum. Assertiveness is a middle response in the behavior spectrum.

When we respond passively, we take care of the needs of others but violate our needs. When we respond aggressively, we take care of our needs but violate the needs of others. It's only when we respond assertively that we take care of our needs *and* the needs of others.

Aggressiveness feels good momentarily. It generates a rush, kind of a "gotcha" feeling. However, this quickly is followed by feelings of uneasiness and guilt. Aggressive people often look to others for confirmation and justification. On the other hand, passiveness is followed by feelings of resentment. The passive person may seek revenge in subtle ways, such as by forgetting, being late, or not understanding. Both passive and aggressive behaviors stem from feelings of low self-esteem and generate new feelings of low self-esteem.

While we all respond in each of these three styles at times, we tend to have a predominant style of relating. Notice that when we act differently, we feel differently. In order to feel differently, we begin by behaving differently.

Assertiveness is a way of expression that is open and honest, but caring. We can express even strong feelings in such a way that we maintain and even improve relationships. When conflicts arise they're much more likely to be resolved satisfactorily when we respond assertively.

Out of fear of negative consequences people tend to bottle up their feelings until they can't stand it. Then they let out their accumulated frustration, resentment, and anger all at one time, "dumping" on people. Then they feel bad and decide never again to say how they feel. This sets up a cycle of repressing, exploding, feeling guilty, working harder to repress, and on and on. But it's *how* we express ourselves that makes the difference.

For instance if a friend is so loud that you can't hear the person you're talking with on the phone, you can seethe and say nothing (passive). Or, you can yell, *"Shut up!"* (aggressive). Or, you can tell your friend how you feel and why it's important to you (assertive). *"I'm really frustrated with the noise you're making. I'm trying to talk with my boss."*

This is called an "I" message, and it's an important technique in learning to speak assertively. Although an "I" message doesn't guarantee a change in behavior, it increases our chances. Most people respond positively when others express themselves sincerely and with respect. However, be prepared. Some people don't. While they agree that being assertive is the only way to be, they don't mean *with them.* A person's response is his or her responsibility, not ours. *Not* dealing assertively with people usually only leads to more problems later.

An "I" message consists of three parts. The *first* part of the "I" message *describes how you feel as a result of the person's behavior.* Taking responsibility for your feelings provides important information for the relationship. This not only may clear up present problems, but also may prevent future misunderstandings.

The *second* part of the "I" message *describes the person's behavior*. Be specific. Rather than saying that a person is an inconsiderate slob, say *"This is the second time in two days that I've had to clean the bathroom after you."*

The *third* part of the "I" message *explains why it's important to you*. People can't understand if you won't tell them what is important to you.

Here are examples of "I" messages:

> *"I feel humiliated when you criticize me in front of people because it seems like you don't respect me."*

> *"I feel hurt when you don't call because I wonder if our relationship is important to you."*

> *"I feel angry when you tease me about being over-weight because I've explained how sensitive I am."*

The complete "I" message gives a great deal of information. It requires honesty, vulnerability, and a sense of personal value. It requires a courage born of knowing that the only way to be close to people is to let them know who we are.

Sometimes a well-phrased "I" message solves the problem by itself. We may end up clarifying things for ourselves as well as for the other person. At other times it repairs the downed lines of communication while constructing new ones, helping the message get through.

Assess Your Assertiveness

Draw a circle around the number that best describes your typical response. Most people find that the most honest response is the first one that occurs to them.

Key: 0-Never 1-Sometimes 2-Usually 3-Always

0 1 2 3   1. Do you find it easy to talk to someone you don't know?

0 1 2 3   2. When a friend asks an unreasonable favor, do you say no?

0 1 2 3   3. Do you find that name-calling is a good way to win arguments?

0 1 2 3   4. When you disagree with something said in class, do you say so?

0 1 2 3   5. On a date are you comfortable if there is a lull in the conversation?

0 1 2 3   6. At a restaurant is it easy to decide what to order?

0 1 2 3   7. If someone cuts in line ahead of you, do you object?

0 1 2 3   8. Do you believe that the best defense is a good offense?

0 1 2 3   9. If friends borrow money and don't repay you, do you remind them?

0 1 2 3   10. Do you look at people when you talk to them?

0 1 2 3   11. If you feel you've been treated unfairly by someone, do you say so?

0 1 2 3   12. Do you refuse to go along with your friends when what they do is wrong?

0 1 2 3   13. If friends say things to put you down, do you tell them how you feel?

0 1 2 3   14. Do you often want to continue an argument after the other person wants to stop?

0 1 2 3   15. If your date pressures you, do you say no?

0 1 2 3   16. Do you avoid laughing at jokes you think are in bad taste?

0 1 2 3 17. If someone is rude to you, are you rude in return?

0 1 2 3 18. When someone pays you a compliment, do you know what to say?

0 1 2 3 19. If you have plans and a friend changes them at the last minute to accept a date, do you speak up?

0 1 2 3 20. Do you object if a date or friend drives too fast?

0 1 2 3 21. How often do you tell your deepest feelings to someone you trust?

0 1 2 3 22. When you disagree, do you insist you're right?

0 1 2 3 23. If you feel a teacher has miscalculated your grade, do you discuss it?

0 1 2 3 24. Do you ask others for help?

0 1 2 3 25. Are you able to praise others?

0 1 2 3 26. If people can't decide what they want, do you make decisions for them?

0 1 2 3 27. If someone harasses you, do you stand up for yourself?

0 1 2 3 28. Do you think it's better to talk than to keep quiet about things that bother you?

0 1 2 3 29. Are you able to relax when giving a presentation?

0 1 2 3 30. Do you find a way to get what you want in any situation?

0 1 2 3 31. If your boss asks you to stay late without paying you extra, do you discuss it?

0 1 2 3 32. If you buy a new shirt and discover a flaw, do you return it for a refund?

0 1 2 3 33. Do you ever comment on something a friend does that you think is wrong?

0 1 2 3 34. Do you openly express affection or appreciation?

0 1 2 3 35. Are you critical of other people's opinions when you disagree?

0 1 2 3 36. If you don't have anyone to eat lunch with, do you ask to join someone?

0 1 2 3 37. When people ask if you mind if they smoke, do you say yes when you do?

0 1 2 3 38. Do you invite others to do things rather than waiting to be asked?

0 1 2 3 39. At a party do you leave if things start happening that you don't like?

0 1 2 3 40. If your friends don't like someone, do you speak to that person anyway?

0 1 2 3 41. Do you stick to your goals regardless of what others say?

Scoring

A. ADD your responses for questions: 1, 2, 4, 5, 6, 7, 9, 10, 11, 12, 13, 15, 16, 18, 19, 20, 21, 23, 24, 25, 27, 28, 29, 31, 32, 33, 34, 36, 37, 38, 39, 40, 41

"A" TOTAL_____

B. ADD your responses for questions: 3, 8, 14, 17, 22, 26,

30, 35

"B" TOTAL_____

C. SUBTRACT "B" TOTAL from "A" TOTAL

SCORE_____

If your score is 67-99, you are exceptionally assertive, expressing your feelings appropriately in a variety of situations.

If your score is 34-66, you are frequently assertive while perhaps needing to express your feelings more freely or more appropriately in some situations.

If your score is 0-33, you are rarely assertive and are probably experiencing dissatisfaction in your personal and social relationships.

"I" Messages

Learning to Speak Assertively

A "You" message is the opposite of an "I" message and is usually an aggressive response. "You" messages switch the focus, blaming others or shifting responsibility for what we're experiencing. "You" messages give no information while making assumptions about the other person. "You" messages generate feelings of anger, defensiveness, or guilt and usually lead to an escalation of negativity or an end to the conversation.

By contrast "I" messages create an exchange of positive expectation and trust. They represent a belief that people in relationship will want to do something about a situation when they understand. For this reason "I" messages are most commonly observed in open, healthy, and developing relationships.

This is the model for "I" messages:

I feel_____when _____

because_____ .

Part I

Write a "You" message and an "I" message for these situations:

Example

Situation:

Your boss gives you a low rating on your job evaluation, and it means you won't be considered for a promotion.

"You" message:

"You've never liked me, and you're out to get me!"

"I" message:

"I feel disappointed when I see the low rating you gave me because I thought you were happy with my work."

1. **Situation:**

   Your best friend brags when you're with other people, and it makes you uncomfortable.

   "You" message:

   "I" message:

   I feel _____ when _____

   because _____ .

2. **Situation:**

   A person you've just started with as a peer helper says you aren't helping and don't know what you're doing.

   "You" message:

   "I" message:

   I feel _____ when _____

   because_____ .

3. **Situation:**

As soon as you get on the phone at night, your older brother decides he needs to use it or needs you to do something.

"You" message:

"I" message:

I feel _____ when _____

because_____ .

4. **Situation:**

You and your sister share the use of the family car. You made arrangements to use the car tonight, and she agreed to be home by 7:00 p.m. She arrives home at 7:35 p.m.

"You" message:

"I" message:

I feel _____ when _____

because_____ .

5. **Situation:**

Your girlfriend/boyfriend flirts with other people when you're not around.

"You" message:

"I" message:

I feel _____ when _____

because_____ .

Part II

This time write your "I" message responses in your *own language and style*. Be sure you include the three elements: how you feel, as a result of what behavior, and why it's important to you.

Example

Situation:

Your boss gives you a low rating on your job evaluation, and it means you won't be considered for a promotion.

"I" message:

"I'm disappointed by the low rating I received. I feel good about my work, and I thought you did, too. I would like to discuss what I'm doing wrong because my goal is to become assistant manager."

1. **Situation:**

   Your best friend brags when you're with other people, and it makes you uncomfortable.

   "I" message:

2. **Situation:**

   A person you've just started with as a peer helper says you aren't helping and don't know what you're doing.

   "I" message:

3. **Situation:**

   As soon as you get on the phone at night, your older brother decides he needs to use it or needs you to do something.

   "I" message:

4. **Situation:**

   You and your sister share the use of the family car. You made arrangements to use the car tonight, and she agreed to be home by 7:00 p.m. She arrives home at 7:35 p.m.

   "I" message:

5. **Situation:**

   Your girlfriend /boyfriend flirts with other people when you're not around.

   "I" message:

Styles of Interaction
Passive, Aggressive, and Assertive

Goal

Passive: Avoid conflict
Aggressive: Win or dominate
Assertive: Solve problems

Basic Message

Passive: I'm not important
Aggressive: You're not important
Assertive: We're both important

Self-Esteem

Passive: Low
Aggressive: Low
Assertive: High

Communication

Passive: Indirect, dishonest
Aggressive: Direct, abusive
Assertive: Direct, honest

Problem-Solving

Passive: Problems are avoided
Aggressive: People are attacked
Assertive: Problems are attacked

Success Styles

Passive: I was lucky
Aggressive: I beat everyone
Assertive: I worked hard

Reaction of Self

Passive: Disgust, no respect for self
Aggressive: Righteous at first, guilty later
Assertive: Confident, respect for self

Reaction of Others

Passive: Frustration, anger
Aggressive: Resistance, anger
Assertive: Respect, cooperation

The Body Language
of Assertive Behavior

Handshake. A firm handshake demonstrates confidence and warmth. A limp handshake reflects a lack of confidence. A handshake that is too hard may be seen as a power play.

Body Posture. Face people and display openness, involvement, and confidence. Sit if people are sitting and stand if they're standing. Being on the same level physically signifies being equal in other respects.

Eye Contact. Look at people as you speak using natural, comfortable eye contact. Never allow it to become rigid. Watch that you don't end eye contact when you disagree with the person.

Active Listening. A person who demonstrates active listening also demonstrates the confidence to hear and deal with what is said. A person who either refuses to listen or can't understand demonstrates insecurity and a closed mind.

Personal Space. Recognize that most people have a personal space of about an arm's length around them. Stand or sit appropriately close without violating or exaggerating this space.

Facial Expression. Make sure your facial expression matches your words. If you're angry, don't smile. If you're expressing affection, don't frown.

Voice. A well-modulated voice reflects a calm and confident emotional state. A voice that is too loud may show a loss of control. A voice that is too soft implies a feeling of unimportance. A sarcastic tone guarantees a less than desired result.

Hand Gestures. Natural gestures add emphasis to a message. Over emphatic gestures are usually a sign of aggressiveness. Fidgeting or fiddling with objects communicates a lack of confidence.

An Exercise in Developing Assertiveness

1. List several small, less important areas in your life where you could benefit from being more assertive. Begin practicing in these areas to prepare for being more assertive in the important areas.

2. Describe a recent important situation in which you were dissatisfied with your response.

3. List your reasons (rationalizations) for not being assertive.

4. Decide what you fear. Ask yourself: What is the worst that can happen? Examine your present behavior and the likely consequences.

5. Describe the general pattern: Who, where, what, when, how often.

6. Imagine responding assertively, feeling confident and respectful. Describe your response.

Skills Chart

Make a check mark in a box next to a behavior each time the behavior is demonstrated:

I. Attending Skill

Sits facing the person	❏ ❏ ❏ ❏ ❏
Maintains good eye contact	❏ ❏ ❏ ❏ ❏
Maintains open, available posture	❏ ❏ ❏ ❏ ❏
Appears relaxed	❏ ❏ ❏ ❏ ❏
Gives encouragement, such as nodding head	❏ ❏ ❏ ❏ ❏

II. Empathy Skill

Reflects feelings	❏ ❏ ❏ ❏ ❏
Reflects content	❏ ❏ ❏ ❏ ❏

III. Clarifying/Questioning Skill

Uses clarifying questions or statements	❏ ❏ ❏ ❏ ❏
Asks open questions	❏ ❏ ❏ ❏ ❏
Asks closed questions	❏ ❏ ❏ ❏ ❏

IV. Assertiveness Skill

Uses "I" messages	❏ ❏ ❏ ❏ ❏
Uses "You" messages	❏ ❏ ❏ ❏ ❏

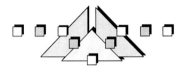

Chapter 6

Confrontation Skill

Confrontation is the fifth skill of peer helping. Confrontation is a loaded word, conjuring images of great emotional wreckage. Many people approach *even the idea* of confrontation by "catastrophizing," meaning they imagine the worst possible outcome.

However, we all have good reason to be apprehensive about confrontation. Have you ever had a bad experience with confrontation? Me too. Sometimes it becomes more of a blowup than a confrontation, and things seem worse than before.

There are two possible explanations. It may be that the person being confronted simply was not willing to accept the information. Or, we may not have handled it well, not knowing or forgetting the guidelines for confrontation.

Confrontation is a blending of assertiveness principles with an understanding of the importance of timing and commitment. Confrontation occurs in all healthy relationships and is the test of the relationship. One way to spot a relationship in trouble is to see that no one cares enough or has courage enough to deal with issues.

We need to have realistic expectations. We can't judge the *value* of confrontation by whether an outcome is positive. It's true that a confrontation well executed increases our chance of success, but there are many variables with confrontation. We must focus on the *process,* rather than the outcome. If the outcome is positive, we can celebrate the relationship. If not, we still have expressed our needs. A relationship that cannot survive an honest but caring expression is guaranteed to bring unhappiness in the long run.

Here are guidelines for effective confrontation:

Commitment to the relationship. The decision to confront needs to be based on a commitment to an ongoing relationship. Otherwise it's probably just an excuse to ventilate feelings or to displace anger.

Timing. The most critical factor is timing, although there is no such thing as the perfect time. A confrontation needs to come as close to the event as possible. If there *is* an ideal time, it's probably when things are going well. But then we say, *"Why spoil things?"* However, people can assimilate what we have to say more easily when they're feeling positive.

Calm, gentle tone of voice. The words of confrontation are powerful, so the tone in which they're said needs to be gentle. This means that a confrontation *never* should occur when you're angry.

Know what you want to say. Plan what to say so you don't get sidetracked. Be precise, concise, and use examples. Talk about your feelings of loss and state what you hope will happen. Never allow yourself to strip a person's dignity by how you express yourself.

Set a time. Allow the person to help choose when the discussion occurs. You've been planning for the confrontation, but the other person wasn't prepared to be on the receiving end. Allow people to say they're not up to it and be willing to defer to the next day if necessary. Be sensitive without allowing yourself to be manipulated.

In private. Always insure privacy. Only those directly involved have any reason to be included. You'll go a long way toward creating positive conditions by seeing that the other person is not put in an unnecessarily defensive position.

Listen. Understand that a person may have shocked or defensive reactions to work through. Be alert to new information that gives you a different perspective or better understanding. Listen closely for any expression of needs from the other person.

Work to reach a shared solution. Decide together what you've learned. Acknowledge areas of misunderstanding. Make a clear and specific statement of what each will do differently and what you hope to accomplish.

Unresolved conflict undermines more relationships than any other single factor. A confrontation from the heart cherishes the relationship. We learn that how we experience the world is our responsibility.

I Will Do You No Favor

If I withhold
my voice of anger from you
for your sake,
In listening too hard to me,
you will hear more anger
than ever any real voice of mine
would have held.
All that I withhold
diminishes me
and cheats you.
All that you withhold
diminishes you
and cheats me.
When we hold back ourselves
for each other's sake,
We do no service
to us either one.
We conspire only
in the weakening of us both.

Author Unknown
Condensed and Revised

Rules for Fighting Fair
Because all is not fair in love and war

Avoid name-calling. One of the fastest ways to humiliate is to use name-calling or other hostile language. It is both demeaning and disrespectful. Finger pointing and other aggressive behaviors are just other forms of name-calling using body language.

Avoid generalizations. Nothing in human behavior is *never* or *always* true. Avoid statements such as, *"You never think of anyone else"* or *"You always ruin everything."* Be specific in your language and give examples to help the other person understand your concern.

Avoid comparisons. It is faulty thinking to compare one human being to another. We are all different, and we need our differences to be accepted. The worst abuses of this occur in families where brothers and sisters are compared to each other.

Avoid the stockpiling /dumping cycle. It's a sure sign this is happening when someone says, *"And furthermore...."* Deal with one issue at a time and do it as close to the event as possible.

Avoid asking why. Rather than asking people why they did something, simply state how you feel about what happened. Asking why is usually a rather effective device for reminding people of their inadequacies.

Avoid interruptions. One of the best ways to contribute to misunderstanding is to interrupt others before they've had an opportunity to complete their statements.

Avoid random fighting. If the situation has deteriorated to the point that you're continually fighting, make an appointment to fight with each other. This prevents negative habits such as nagging or fault finding from developing. It also builds in periods of neutrality.

Own your feelings. Never let the heat of the moment convince you that your feelings are someone else's responsibility. Say, *"I am angry,"* not *"You make me angry."* Check your assumptions about a person's feelings. Just because you've known a person a long time doesn't mean you know what he or she is thinking or feeling now.

Take responsibility for change. It's a rare situation when the responsibility lies with one person. There are two sides, or more, to every situation. We all contribute to the development of a problem in our own way.

Develop signals. Agree in advance on signals to alert the other person of a problem. For example, you can agree to raise your hand each time someone interrupts. Signals allow people to take care of their needs in the discussion without resorting to walking away or other disruptive behaviors. A "T" for time out can signal that you've reached your limit. Decide together when the conversation will resume.

Know the issue. Be sure you know what you're fighting about. Ask yourselves if the fight is about the presented issue or if there's an underlying issue. In couple relationships in particular, fights are frequently over something other than the stated issue.

Know what you hope to achieve. People frequently can give a long list of things they want someone to stop doing without being able to name one thing they want him or her to start doing. Be prepared to suggest a new way of relating.

Helper Confrontation

Helper confrontation is different from confrontation in relationship. In personal confrontation, we point to behaviors that are causing *us* a problem. In helper confrontations, we point to discrepancies that are causing *them* a problem.

The guideline for helper confrontation is: the stronger the relationship, the stronger the confrontation. This means that confrontation is premature if you've just begun a helper relationship. Empathy and genuine concern must be established over a period of time before a helping relationship will survive confrontation. Then the opportunity for people to see that *what they're saying is not what they're doing* can be the key to awareness.

Helper confrontations can be passive, aggressive, or assertive. The assertive helper response is the only one that gently points to discrepancies between words and actions.

Give a passive, aggressive, and assertive helper response to each situation:

Example

Friend:

"Things are going really well with Jason and me. He never has time to talk or do anything with me anymore, but we're doing a lot better."

Helper (Passive):

"I'm glad things are so good between you."

Helper (Aggressive):

"Which of us are you trying to fool?"

Helper (Assertive):

"You say that things are better, but you sound sad to me. It seems that your relationship with Jason is still unsettled."

1. Friend:

"My parents are getting along great. Oh sure, they still fight. As a matter of fact, they had a real blowout last night! But it's good now."

Helper (Passive):

Helper (Aggressive):

Helper (Assertive):

2. Friend:

"I don't have a drinking problem. I never drink before lunch, and the only time I get drunk is on the weekend."

Helper (Passive):

Helper (Aggressive):

Helper (Assertive):

3. Friend:

"I just found out my boyfriend cheated on me for the third time. He felt so bad though that I just know he won't do it again."

Helper (Passive):

Helper (Aggressive):

Helper (Assertive):

4. **Friend:**

   "I deserved an A on that paper. I worked with Bob, and he got an A. Sure he did more research and stuff like that. But I worked almost as hard, and I got a lousy C!"

   Helper (Passive):

   Helper (Aggressive):

   Helper (Assertive):

5. **Friend:**

   "She's spreading rumors about me again. I give her the dirtiest look I can when I see her. I won't play her games. I'll just keep ignoring her!"

   Helper (Passive):

   Helper (Aggressive):

   Helper (Assertive):

Is there an area of your life that would benefit from confrontation? Write a passive, aggressive, and assertive response to yourself:

Situation:

(Passive)

(Aggressive)

(Assertive)

Skills Chart

Make a check mark in a box next to a behavior each time the behavior is demonstrated:

I. Attending Skill

Sits facing the person ❏ ❏ ❏ ❏ ❏

Maintains good eye contact ❏ ❏ ❏ ❏ ❏

Maintains open, available posture ❏ ❏ ❏ ❏ ❏

Appears relaxed ❏ ❏ ❏ ❏ ❏

Gives encouragement, such as nodding head ❏ ❏ ❏ ❏ ❏

II. Empathy Skill

Reflects feelings ❏ ❏ ❏ ❏ ❏

Reflects content ❏ ❏ ❏ ❏ ❏

III. Clarifying/Questioning Skill

Uses clarifying questions or statements ❏ ❏ ❏ ❏ ❏

Asks open questions ❏ ❏ ❏ ❏ ❏

Asks closed questions ❏ ❏ ❏ ❏ ❏

IV. Assertiveness Skill

Uses "I" messages ❏ ❏ ❏ ❏ ❏

Uses "You" messages ❏ ❏ ❏ ❏ ❏

V. Confrontation Skill

Is non-confrontative ❏ ❏ ❏ ❏ ❏

Uses aggressive confrontation ❏ ❏ ❏ ❏ ❏

Uses assertive confrontation ❏ ❏ ❏ ❏ ❏

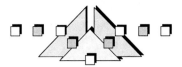

Chapter 7

Problem-Solving Skill

The sixth skill of peer helping is that of *problem solving.* Problem solving is discussed last because it should be used last. All the other skills are necessary to build the foundation for problem solving. When used effectively and in sequence, the other skills naturally lead into solution seeking.

Problem solving occurs only when people *feel worthwhile* and when *they understand* their feelings and responses within a situation. Problem solving happens only when people see their choices and *accept their responsibility*. It is only within this framework that effective solutions are found.

Then the process begins with a plan of action. A plan requires us to focus on the situation, on ourselves, and on a desirable solution.

Steps for Developing a Plan of Action

Identify the specifics. Be clear on the problem. Look at your feelings and responses within the situation. Consider the elements of the problem: Who, what, where, when, how often. Decide how the problem situation is different from your ideal situation.

Brainstorm alternatives. Focus on the choices within your control. Look at what *you* can begin doing differently, not what you wish the world would do differently. Generate a list of alternatives that includes every response you could make, even those that seem impossible or unrealistic.

Consider the consequences of each alternative. Since everything you do (cause) has its consequence (effect), decide which cause-and-effect combination you're willing to experience. It sometimes helps to make a list of *pro's* and *con's*.

Make a contract. Write down your intention and plan of action. Include the steps to be taken, the obstacles to be overcome, and a target date. Share your plan of action with an accountability partner.

Do it. All the planning in the world will get you nowhere if you don't take action. Your choice is to live with it or to take steps to create an environment or relationship of greater joy and satisfaction.

Evaluate your plan. Continue to adjust or even revise the plan of action to keep pace with your perception of the situation. Problem solving is not static. It's dynamic. It's a constantly developing process.

Personal Priorities

Making daily decisions as well as major life decisions requires that you are clear on what is important to you. Arrange the priorities listed below in order of their importance in *your* life. Put a "1" next to your highest priority, a "2" next to the second, and so on.

_____ CREATIVITY (expressing ideas or talents)

_____ EXCITEMENT (interest and stimulation)

_____ FUN (having the time of your life)

_____ INTEGRITY (honesty and honor)

_____ KNOWLEDGE (wisdom and awareness)

_____ LOVE (family and friends)

_____ MONEY (financial security)

_____ PERSONAL GROWTH (process of becoming)

_____ PHYSICAL DEVELOPMENT (healthy body)

_____ PURPOSE (meaning and contribution)

_____ POWER (ability to influence others)

_____ RECOGNITION (acknowledgment of others)

_____ SERENITY (surrender and peace of mind)

_____ SERVICE (sharing skills and resources)

_____ SPIRITUALITY (connectedness)

Our priorities are part of our evolving growth, and they may be different at different times in our lives. Since each of these priorities is important to a well-balanced life, this list can be seen as a directory of characteristics to be developed in a lifetime, rather than as a choice for or against.

No-Lose Problem Solving

We approach too much of life with an *"I win, you lose"* attitude. In relationships the problem with being a winner is then there's a loser, who might want to be the winner next time. This sets up a destructive and unnecessary condition in a relationship.

For example, let's say you and I are trying to decide where we'll go for dinner. I want Mexican food and you want Italian food. I refuse to have Italian food and insist on having Mexican food. You agree. This is a *win-lose solution* and is an example of aggressive/passive problem solving.

Or, we might decide that *both of us lose.* The message here is that if I can't have what I want, then you can't have what you want either. So when I refuse to have Italian food, you refuse to have Mexican food. Neither one of us is willing to have what the other wants, so we end up having a cold sandwich at the supermarket deli. This is a *no-win solution* and is an example of aggressive problem solving.

However, *no-win solutions* also take the form of passive problem solving. When you asked me where I'd like to go for dinner, I may have said, *"I don't know. Where do you want to go?"* And you could have said, *"I don't know. Where do you want to go?"*

There is—thank goodness—another way. It's to find a solution that satisfies both. Sometimes it involves compromise: When I want Mexican food and you want Italian food, we might have Italian food this time and Mexican food next time. Other times it involves a more imaginative approach: We might find a fun little restaurant bazaar where they serve several kinds of food in the same location. Or, we might remind ourselves that we've been meaning to experiment, and we could try that great looking new Chinese restaurant. These are called *no-lose solutions* and are examples of assertive problem solving.

Here are the steps to no-lose solutions:

Decide that you want a no-lose relationship. Decide that you want a relationship based on equality of needs, feelings, and wants. Remember too that *giving* is not the same as *giving-in*. To love is to want the best for the other person.

Understand the disagreement. Make sure you each understand what the other person is feeling and thinking. When you understand and care what another person is experiencing, the solution to the disagreement begins to develop naturally.

Clarify your understanding. If you see connections between this situation and others that have occurred, spend some time discussing this. A disagreement, which seems like the worst thing that could happen, can lead to a deeper bond between people becoming the best thing that could happen.

Brainstorm solutions. Have fun with this. Be crazy. Laughter is healing and can get us over the roughest places. However, laughter is a double-edged sword. Be sure you're laughing *at* yourself but *with* others. Let your imaginations go in developing this list. Show your appreciation of the other person through the solutions you suggest.

Pick one. Choose the one that seems to satisfy best at the time. It's often not the solution itself, but the deepened understanding and commitment that are the true victories. Re-evaluate your decision periodically to consider adjustments. Relationships are constantly evolving so decisions affecting them also need to evolve.

Goals
If you don't know where you're going, how will you know when you get there?

Select your goal. Know what you want. We often don't get what we want because we haven't decided what that is. Choose something you would like to change, have, or improve.

Picture your goal. Consider what it will mean to have met your goal. How will your life be different? What will you have gained? What will you have lost? Count the cost.

Write down your goal. Write a description of your ideal situation including the details of what it will take to get there.

Select sub-goals. If your goal is a long-term one, divide it into short-term goals. Decide what you need to do today, next week, next month, next year, and so on. Use short-term goals to signal your progress toward your major goal. If you fail to accomplish a goal, don't criticize. Instead choose a new goal or renew your dedication to the original one.

Limit yourself. Don't try to do too much. You'll find that you're most effective if you focus on one major goal at a time. Once you're experiencing progress toward your major goal, you can move on to new areas. If you get discouraged, simplify your goal. Goals point you in the direction you say you want to go. Make sure you're focused on goals you're willing to work for.

Reward yourself. As you see progress or when you achieve a goal, celebrate it by doing something nice for yourself. As the friend to ourselves that we're learning to be, it's nice to have someone notice.

Skills Chart

Make a check mark in a box next to a behavior each time the behavior is demonstrated:

I. Attending Skill

Sits facing the person ❏ ❏ ❏ ❏ ❏

Maintains good eye contact ❏ ❏ ❏ ❏ ❏

Maintains open, available posture ❏ ❏ ❏ ❏ ❏

Appears relaxed ❏ ❏ ❏ ❏ ❏

Gives encouragement, such as nodding head ❏ ❏ ❏ ❏ ❏

II. Empathy Skill

Reflects feelings ❏ ❏ ❏ ❏ ❏

Reflects content ❏ ❏ ❏ ❏ ❏

III. Clarifying/Questioning Skill

Uses clarifying questions or statements ❏ ❏ ❏ ❏ ❏

Asks open questions ❏ ❏ ❏ ❏ ❏

Asks closed questions ❏ ❏ ❏ ❏ ❏

IV. Assertiveness Skill

Uses "I" messages ❏ ❏ ❏ ❏ ❏

Uses "You" messages ❏ ❏ ❏ ❏ ❏

V. Confrontation Skill

Is non-confrontative ❏ ❏ ❏ ❏ ❏

Uses aggressive confrontation ❏ ❏ ❏ ❏ ❏

Uses assertive confrontation ❏ ❏ ❏ ❏ ❏

VI. Problem-Solving Skill

Facilitates problem identification ❏ ❏ ❏ ❏ ❏

Facilitates list of alternatives ❏ ❏ ❏ ❏ ❏

Facilitates evaluation of consequences ❏ ❏ ❏ ❏ ❏

Facilitates action plan/goal development ❏ ❏ ❏ ❏ ❏

Section III
Topic Development

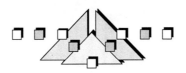

Chapter 8

Suicide Prevention and Intervention

Suicide: Myths or Facts?

T F 1. Suicide is against the law in this state.

T F 2. A person usually commits suicide without warning.

T F 3. Most suicide attempts occur late at night and away from home.

T F 4. It is dangerous to talk about suicide with a depressed person.

T F 5. Use of alcohol and other drugs can increase the risk of suicide.

T F 6. Suicidal people want to die, and they will find a way eventually.

T F 7. More females than males commit suicide.

T F 8. People who talk about suicide rarely do it.

T F 9. Depressed people are the greatest suicidal risks.

T F10. Suicidal people are mentally ill.

T F11. Once people become suicidal, they will be suicidal forever.

T F12. Suicide occurs most often among the poor.

T F13. Suicidal people rarely seek medical attention.

T F14. People who have made one suicide attempt won't make another.

T F15. Suicide rates are increasing among the young.

Suicide: The Facts

1. Suicide is not against the law in most states. This can severely limit the ability of law enforcement and social agencies to intervene.

2. Although suicide is sometimes impulsive, it's usually planned well in advance and then hinted at or actually communicated to others.

3. Most suicide attempts take place in the home, often in the late afternoon or early evening, when friends and family are most likely to intervene.

4. Allowing people to talk about suicidal thoughts provides relief and a sense of being understood. This is a strong deterrent because it encourages ventilation of feelings and a frank discussion of the problem.

5. Use of alcohol and other drugs vastly reduces the fear of death. Over 50 percent of teens that committed suicide had been using alcohol or other drugs.

6. Suicidal people are ambivalent about life. They don't want to die, but they're not sure they want to live. They're more anti-life than pro-death. Teens in particular usually want to be rescued but don't know how to ask for help. They sometimes will just gamble with death.

7. Although females attempt suicide three times as often as males, males kill themselves four times as often as females.

8. Most people who kill themselves have hinted at suicide or have told someone they were going to kill themselves.

9. Depression is such a draining emotion that it immobilizes people. The greatest danger comes during the three months after people recover from a deep depression. This is when they have the energy to carry out a plan.

10. Normal people kill themselves every day. Although a small percentage of suicidal people are mentally ill, most suicidal people just feel hopeless. They simply haven't been able to find another way to stop the pain.

11. Most people are suicidal only for a limited time. If they're given support and assistance, most lead normal lives and never again experience a suicidal crisis.

12. Suicide isn't limited to any particular economic status. It occurs proportionately among all levels of society.

13. It's estimated that over 50 percent of suicidal people had visited a physician for nonspecific medical attention within three to six months of killing themselves.

14. About half of those who try once will try again. Four out of five people who kill themselves already have made at least one attempt.

15. Suicide is now the third leading cause of death for youth between the ages of 15 and 24 years and the sixth leading cause of death for those between the ages of 5 and 14 years.

Suicide

The Ultimate Tragedy

About 5,000 teens and young adults kill themselves every year in this country. Suicide falls behind unintentional injury and homicide as the three leading causes of death among 15- to 24-year-olds. The rate of teen suicide has nearly tripled since the 1950s. For every suicide attempt that succeeds, there are an estimated 100 that do not. While more females attempt suicide, more males die because of their lethal methods.

Most people think about suicide at some point in their lives. These thoughts are normal. However, why do so many teens today act upon these thoughts? Adolescence is a time of turbulence, change, and transition. Teens face a vast array of challenges ranging from new social roles and relationships to biological and physical changes at a time when they're called to make decisions about the future. The stress, confusion, and self-doubt create feelings of insecurity and inadequacy. Adolescence is born of loss—the loss of childhood. This has always been so, but today additional losses are added.

Because of cultural and moral changes, teens today find themselves struggling with new freedoms and social pressures, but often without a strong foundation from which to respond. Many *parents* also are dealing with upheaval and are establishing new lives. So some teens contend with new homes, new schools, new friends, and even new parents. Although this can be done if teens feel loved and cherished, many find themselves in the way and cast aside. This leads to a new and profound loss, that of *not belonging*. When this is compounded by any new loss, the result can be devastating.

Teens today also experience increased financial and social complexities along with the pressure to succeed. The American dream of living the good life often starts with pressure to get into the best college and to choose the right career. Yet, the right career today may be obsolete tomorrow.

When the pressure to fit in, to look right, and to make the right decisions is compounded by the uncertainties of life, some teens consider death as a solution. Yet, when teens speak of their pressures, many adults say, *"But these are the best times of your life!"* The teen thinks, *"You mean it gets worse?"* Suicide becomes a way to escape conflicts and pressures that seem overwhelming.

Teens may not have the perspective of knowing that these problems will pass. They tend to view temporary situations as permanent. The media has added to this problem. Many teens grow up watching life's problems reduced to a 30- to 60-minute formula on television. They've come to expect an immediate solution to every problem. Some teens simply are not equipped emotionally to work through difficult situations, and death becomes an alternative to them.

Young people who are this deeply distressed usually will give warning signs. Each warning sign is indicative of trouble and needs to be dealt with by a frank statement of concern. When several warning signs occur simultaneously, intervention *must* occur. The warning signs of impending suicide include but are not limited to:

1. Talking or hinting about suicide, including having made a previous suicide gesture or attempt.
2. Personality changes, such as an aggressive person becoming passive or a passive person becoming aggressive.
3. Sudden changes in eating or sleeping patterns, such as overeating or loss of appetite, inability to sleep or sleeping all the time.
4. A dramatic drop in school performance and/or a sudden disinterest in personal appearance.
5. Themes of suicide or death in stories, poems, or other works of art.
6. Withdrawal from family, friends, and normal activities.
7. Listening to the same sad songs over and over or listening to music with angry, violent themes.
8. A sudden unexplained happy mood after a period of depression.
9. Making a will or giving away prized possessions never shared before.
10. Purchasing a gun, knife, rope, or other type of weapon including alcohol or other drugs.

What should you do if someone you know fits this description? Always take any mention of suicide seriously, no matter how often you've heard it. One of the most dangerous and popularly accepted myths is that people who talk about suicide never do it. *Wrong!* Most people talk about it beforehand. Don't fall into the trap of thinking that such talk is just for attention. *Of course it's for attention.* More importantly, it's a cry for help. People don't resort to this way of asking for help when they know another way.

Openly but gently express your concern by describing the person's *behavior.* Be specific in your observations without analyzing. Ask if they've been thinking about suicide. Don't be afraid that you'll be giving them ideas. The person considering suicide *already has the idea.*

A person in this much pain will be grateful for your sensitivity and relieved to talk about it. People who aren't thinking of suicide won't begin thinking about it because you brought it up. However, they certainly will see their behavior from a new perspective and appreciate your concern for them.

Encourage the person to talk. Show your concern by listening intently with deep acceptance and understanding. The more you help people to express their pain, the further they'll move from the idea of suicide.

However, this is *not* enough to insure that a person will remain safe. You're an important part of this support system, but you must never take full responsibility. This is a secret that can't be kept, and it's a secret the person actually doesn't want kept. *Sometimes we have to risk a friendship to save a friend.*

It's a sad fact that most young people are resistant to the idea of involving adults. If you ever ask yourself the question, *"Should I tell an adult?"* remember the answer is *Yes!* Know the referral system within your program and use it. *Don't be the last person someone talked to about suicide.*

A professional in your school or community *must* notify the family. It's sometimes hard for teens to accept that parents will be notified because they often believe the parents are a big part of the problem. People often handle emergencies better than the daily hassles of living. Parents are no exception. Most parents simply don't realize how bad it's been for their son or daughter. They deserve and *must* be given the chance to help.

It helps to remember that most people don't want to die. They just want the pain to stop. You can be an important part of helping a friend choose life.

Techniques of Assessment and Intervention

Assessment:

Handle (HNDL) Assessment Technique:

H How *handy* or available is the weapon?

N How *near* is help?

D How *detailed* or specific is the plan?

L How *lethal* is the method?

Questions to ask:

❑ Has it been so bad that you've been thinking about suicide?

❑ How long have you been thinking about suicide?

❑ How often do you think about suicide?

❑ Have you decided how you would do it?

❑ Have you decided when you would do it?

❑ What has kept you from doing it so far?

❑ Why now?

❑ Have you ever tried to kill yourself before?

Caution: If they are drinking, using, responses are unreliable.

Intervention:

1. Establish a relationship by listening.
2. Encourage them to express feelings.
3. Accept what is said without shock.
4. Identify problems without dwelling on them.
5. Identify positive alternatives.
6. Avoid the shock and pain of family and friends. This is sometimes the motive.
7. Express the loss of their life as being a loss for you, if genuine.
8. Learn what is meaningful and offer hope. Don't offer what you can't deliver.
9. Make a no-suicide contract.
10. Call your crisis intervention program. Stay with the person until help arrives.

No-Suicide Contract

I _____ promise that I will not kill or hurt myself, accidentally or on purpose, from now until _____ when I agree to talk to my counselor, _____ .

I agree to give everything I would use to kill or hurt myself including_____ to_____ .

I also agree that if I start thinking about killing or hurting myself, I will talk to _____ my counselor at _____ or

my friend_____at _____ or

the crisis intervention program at _____ .

Signed: _____

Witnessed:_____

Dated:_____

Levels of Suicidal Risk

Level I Risk

Some indicators of developing trouble:

A. Mild depression

B. Unusual aggressive or passive behavior

C. Alcohol or substance abuse

D. Changes in eating or sleeping habits

E. Drop in school performance and/or lack of interest in personal appearance

F. Family strife or impending divorce

G. Other recent loss or crisis

Characteristics: People at this stage are frequently communicating double messages, saying they're not thinking about suicide while their behavior suggests otherwise. They have no clear plan, no definite time frame, and no readily available method as yet. However, they're depressed and focused on death.

Example: People who write morbid poems or stories about death or who jokingly talk about suicide.

Intervention:

No-Suicide contract

Referral to counselor

Parent notification

Follow-up

Level II Risk

Some indicators of developing risk:

A. Chronic depression

B. Abrupt changes in personality or sudden mood swings

C. Impulsive or extreme risk-taking behavior

D. Inability to concentrate

E. Withdrawal from friends, family, and activities

F. Change in family status or a move to a new school

Characteristics:

People at this stage are still ambivalent about suicide, but they may have a vague plan or a plan that is not highly lethal. They will not yet have set a definite time or conceived a readily available and highly lethal method. However, they're now mentally trying out the idea of suicide.

Example: A girl who says she just might take any pills in her medicine cabinet the next time things get really bad.

Intervention:

No-suicide contract

Referral to counselor

Parent notification

Professional assessment and assistance

Follow-up

Level III Risk

Some indicators of severe risk:

A. Acute depression

B. Talk of helplessness, hopelessness, haplessness

C. Talk of being dead

D. Making a will or giving away possessions

E. Suicidal gestures

F. Loss of an important person or loss of status

G. Failure to achieve long sought goal

H. Trouble with authorities

I. Purchasing a weapon

J. Previous suicide attempt

Characteristics:

People at this stage have made a definite plan and set a definite time. They have a readily available and highly lethal method. They often will begin subtly saying good-bye to people, perhaps by visiting a grandparent or someone they haven't seen for awhile.

Example: A guy who has a gun in his closet and has decided that Saturday when the family is out of town, he's going to use it.

Intervention:

Restrain if possible but *never* try to take away a weapon

Call 911

Parent notification

Professional assessment and assistance

Follow-up

Note: People may not work through the levels of suicidal risk in order. It's possible for the first indication of trouble to show itself in Level III characteristics. It's also possible for a person to go from Level I to Level III in a very short time. Your job is not to take responsibility for people but to *get them to help.*

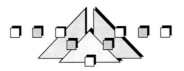

Chapter 9

Alcoholism

The Elephant in the Living Room

The American Council on Alcoholism estimates that over 20 million people in the United States abuse alcohol or are alcoholic. It's estimated that a problem drinker affects as many as six other people on average. This means 120 million people are negatively affected by alcohol in this country, including some of your acquaintances or friends—and perhaps your family or yourself.

Alcoholism is a primary, chronic, progressive, potentially fatal disease:

- It's a *primary* disease because it *is the problem* and not just a symptom of a problem. By the time problem drinking reaches the stage of alcoholism, it has taken on the properties and dynamics of a disease. Attempts to treat alcoholism simply by treating underlying problems have been notably unsuccessful.

- It's a *chronic* disease because no one who has become alcoholic has ever ceased to be alcoholic. Alcoholism can be treated, but it can't be cured. A recovering alcoholic can never safely use alcohol again.

- It's a *progressive* disease because there are stages in the development of alcoholism. If left untreated, it gets worse.

- It's a *potentially fatal* disease. People drink themselves to death, either quickly through an overdose (called alcohol poisoning) or slowly by degeneration of organs such as the liver, kidneys, pancreas, heart, and brain. Or, they may be killed in a car accident while driving under the influence. Without treatment, alcoholism invariably leads to premature death.

A person born into an alcoholic family has inherited a genetic predisposition toward the development of alcoholism. More than half of all alcoholics have an alcoholic parent. An alcoholic metabolizes alcohol differently, meaning that the body *uses* it differently. It's not when or how much people drink but what happens when they drink that indicates a problem.

These are the progressive steps to alcoholism:

1. You have begun to drink.

You find that alcohol serves a friendly social purpose. You have a few beers or some wine now and then. Once in a while you have too much, but in the morning you can't stand the thought of alcohol. After the hangover you're fine. Most people never go past this point. Others move to the next step.

2. You experience a growing preoccupation.

You begin anticipating your periods of drinking. You look forward to the next party or "kegger," or you use softball leagues or camping trips as an excuse for heavy drinking. If there isn't drinking, you aren't interested. Your tolerance increases, and you take pride in drinking everyone "under the table."

3. You start having blackouts.

You are getting drunk regularly. You're one of a crowd that likes to drink hard. You believe you can stop any time, and then it happens. You drink your usual, but later you *can't remember* anything after a certain time. It's gone from your memory. You didn't pass out; you had a blackout. A blackout is a chemically-induced amnesia, sometimes lasting for several hours. People behave normally during a blackout, but later they can't remember anything that happened. A blackout is an electrical imbalance in the brain caused by alcohol and is a warning sign of developing alcoholism.

4. You find alcohol means more to you than to others.

You gulp your drinks now. You want that kick more than ever, and you begin sneaking drinks. During a party you take a few extras when nobody's looking, or you have a couple before you get to the party. You can stop if you recognize what's happening. If not, your chances of becoming an alcoholic are high.

_____ *danger* _____

5. You are drinking more than you intend.

Almost every time you take a drink, you drink more than you had planned. You go to a party determined to have just two drinks, and you wind up drunk without knowing how it happened. You can no longer control the amount you drink.

6. You start excusing your drinking.

You make excuses for your loss of control. You tell yourself it's been a bad day. It's someone's birthday. You had a fight with your parents, boss, teachers, girlfriend, boyfriend, or neighbor. There's always a reason why you drink too much. The fact is you feel guilty, and you've begun to lie to yourself and others.

7. You take "eye-openers."

You begin taking a drink in the morning to get started. You take it as a kind of medicine, and you tell yourself you need it. You're a little shaky from the night before. The drink eases your conscience and lifts your ego. It also strengthens the self-deceit that is making you more and more dependent.

8. You begin to drink alone.

Not long after you start drinking in the morning, you begin drinking alone. You drink to escape into the private, distorted world of your imagination—a world where you tell off your boss or parents, amaze your friends with your brilliance, or become a great poet or financial whiz. What you cannot see is that drinking has become a flight from reality.

9. You become antisocial.

Solitary drinking already is antisocial. However, you take it a step further. You pick fights with strangers. You smash things. You pull practical jokes. You become self-conscious and wary, imagining that people are staring or whispering. Drinking has distorted your judgment. Your remedy is more alcohol.

_____ *danger* _____

10. You go on benders.

The acute stage of your drinking begins. You are an alcoholic. You drink blindly, helplessly, with one goal: to get drunk. You disregard family, friends, job, even food and shelter. You'll lie, pawn your possessions, and steal to get more alcohol. You may become frightened and go "on the wagon." This works if you stay on it, but you only plan to quit for a time. You do it to prove that you *can quit*. But you can't quit because you don't intend to quit.

11. You experience repeated harmful consequences.

It's beginning to crash in on you now. You've got family trouble. You've got legal trouble, with traffic violations or charges of drunk and disorderly. You've lost your friends and your associations within the community. You've been passed over at work, and your job is on the line.

12. You know deep remorse and resentment.

You have sober moments when you feel deep remorse. Working against this though is the deep-seated conviction that you have good reasons, but nobody understands. You begin to resent people. You have fits of rage over little things or nothing at all. A friend forgets to call, someone leaves a bike in the driveway, you recall a remark made last week, and you become furious.

13. You feel deep, nameless anxiety.

The steps to emotional and spiritual bankruptcy are coming faster and closer. You feel a vague but ever present fear. It shows in your trembling hands, vacant stares, and jittery nerves. People call it "the shakes." It's as much an expression of your fear as it is a physical reaction.

14. You realize your drinking has beaten you.

The day comes when you admit you can't handle alcohol. Perhaps you've awakened in the hospital or in jail. You finally accept that you're powerless over alcohol and your life has become unmanageable.

15. You get help or go under.

You face the ultimate choice: get help or give up. You've thrown away love, respect, and security. Your only comfort—alcohol—has proved false. Recovery requires truth, plus time, surrender, and the support of many others. The alternative is to stay where you are until you die. Hope lies in facing the truth and asking for help.

Alcoholism also deeply affects the family of the alcoholic. Alcoholism is a *family disease*, called *codependency*. Codependency becomes a primary coping disease within each family member.

Codependency is a preoccupation with feeling responsible for the behavior and the welfare of another human being. The codependent becomes *addicted* to trying to control the thoughts, feelings, and behavior of another person.

In the chemically dependent family, the family members adapt to the dependent in whatever way gives them some protection from the pain. Unfortunately, this generally means two things are happening. One is that people are repressing their feelings. The other is that they're becoming locked into a set of rigid survival roles. The longer people use a particular survival role to cope the more addicted they become, eventually identifying themselves *as the role*.

In *Another Chance: Hope and Health for the Alcoholic Family,* Sharon Wegscheider (1981) identified the survival roles that develop within the alcoholic family. The members of the family find—or are given—these survival roles as their way of dealing with the pain.

The first survival role is that of *chief enabler,* which is usually the spouse or parent. However, each family member participates in the process of enabling. There's a significant difference between helping and enabling. Helping is what we do to provide an effective solution to a problem. *Enabling* is what we do to allow a problem to continue.

Alcoholism is the elephant in the living room. The family members all navigate around it, but no one talks about it or admits that it is there.

The chief enabler is the person closest to the dependent. As the dependent becomes less and less responsible, the chief enabler becomes more and more responsible. Eventually the chief enabler may be doing all the parenting in the family plus taking a second job to help with the finances. The chief enabler is the one who provides the excuses to the neighbors, the family, and the dependent's boss.

All of the chief enabler's efforts are designed to keep the family together. However, what chief enablers don't realize is that they're actually making matters worse by providing a buffer between the dependent and the consequences of his or her actions. One of the most difficult things for chief enablers to recognize is that they have become *part of the problem.*

The defenses the chief enabler chooses are those of super-responsibility and super-competence to cover up feelings of fear, guilt, anger, and self-pity. The role of the chief enabler is to provide responsibility for the family.

The next survival role is that of the firstborn child, the *hero.* This child comes into the family and quickly senses the chaos and undercurrents—*and feels responsible.* This child thinks that if only he was a better son or she was a better daughter, this wouldn't be happening. So the hero learns to cope by being very, very good.

The hero provides esteem for the family through achievement. However, the hero also experiences tremendous frustration and inadequacy. Because of the progressive nature of the disease of alcoholism, as the hero accomplishes more and more, the situation becomes worse and worse. No matter how much the hero does or achieves, it's never enough. That's because the hero is trying to *fix* a situation for which a child has no responsibility or control.

As a child the hero will function as a "little adult." During later years the hero will be the student who is distressed at any score less than perfect. As an adult the hero will be involved with numerous committees, clubs, and activities and be known for not being able to say no.

Even with all the frustration and stress, the hero is very hard to intervene upon because of the success and high profile achievement. Any statement of concern is likely to be met with, *"Me? What could be wrong? Look how successful I am."*

The defenses the hero chooses are those of achievement, responsibility, and an "I've got it together" attitude to cover up feelings of fear, inadequacy, frustration, guilt, and anger. The role of the hero is to provide worth for the family.

The next survival role is that of the angry, rebellious second child, the *scapegoat*. This child comes into the family and senses the chaos, and at first the scapegoat tries to participate and to compete positively. However, the scapegoat has two distinct disadvantages. It's always difficult, at least in the beginning, for a younger child to compete with an older one. But more importantly the *role* of hero has been assigned to the older child, and the scapegoat will never receive the acknowledgment, attention, and praise given to the hero.

What happens when children can't get attention positively? They get it negatively. And that's just what the scapegoat does, at first by throwing temper tantrums and getting into fights at school, in the neighborhood, and at home. This often escalates into ditching school, running away, perhaps getting pregnant, and often becoming chemically dependent.

The defenses the scapegoat chooses are those of rebellious-ness, sullenness, and stubbornness to cover up feelings of anger, loneliness, rejection, and pain. The role of the scape-goat is to provide distraction for the family.

The next survival role is that of the *lost child.* This child senses the dynamics of the family and, like the scapegoat, the lost child feels like an outsider. Instead of resorting to the acting-out behaviors of the scapegoat, this child adapts by "getting lost."

The lost child learns that the safest place to be is alone, away from the chaos in the family where this child usually is overlooked anyway. The lost child stays quietly busy with lots of books, pets, projects, but few if any friends. The lost child's deep lack of self-worth comes from years of being overlooked, but at least this is one child the family "doesn't have to worry about."

The defenses the lost child chooses are indifference, busy-ness, and super-independence to cover up feelings of pain, loneliness, worthlessness, grief, and deeply repressed anger. The role of the lost child is to provide welcome relief for the family.

The last survival role is that of the youngest child, the *mas-cot.* The youngest child is the one to bring fun, humor, and diversion to the family. The mascot is clever and charming, but also may be irritating and hyperactive.

The natural tendency of any family to protect the youngest is exaggerated in this family with all its secrets. When the mascot asks if anything is wrong, family members withhold or give misleading information. This creates tremendous con-fusion since the mascot's instincts say something is terribly wrong. Without intervention, mascots will carry an inability to trust their instincts into every relationship of their lives.

However, what mascots learn is that they can control the fam-ily scene, or any other stressful situation, for as long as they can hold the floor. This is the person whose only technique for dealing with pain and stress is humor and clowning.

The defenses the mascot chooses are fun, clowning, and an "anything for a laugh" attitude to cover up feelings of fear, confusion, anxiety, and insecurity. The role of the mascot is to provide fun and humor for the family.

It's important to note that these survival roles also may occur in dysfunctional families *without* chemical dependency. Any time the focus is on one person and everyone else "walks on eggs," these dynamics may be created. Some examples include a workaholic parent, a parent or sibling with severe illness or disability, or a parent with unresolved control or rage issues.

People sometimes will take more than one role, becoming a blend of two or more roles. People also may take different roles at different times in their lives. When an older sibling leaves home or goes off to college, this often stimulates a reshuffling of roles. That is until the older sibling returns home for holidays or vacations at which time the original roles often are reassigned.

In another variation if there are five or more years between siblings, the roles often are repeated. This can result in a family of heroes.

Alcoholism is a problem affecting millions of people, including perhaps your family, your friends, or yourself. So what can you do if someone you love is chemically dependent?

Until recently it was generally accepted that the dependent had to "hit bottom" and ask for help before anything could be done. However, by waiting until the crisis came, it was often too late to salvage much of life. Now through a process called intervention, it's possible for those who care about the dependent to *create a crisis*. This has the same effect for the dependent as hitting bottom, but without having to wait until all is lost. Alcoholics Anonymous, or AA, calls this "hitting a high bottom."

An intervention, which should occur only under the direction of a professional, *unites* the significant people in the dependent's life. The intervention is a presentation to the dependent consisting of statements written by each person describing specific times the dependent's behavior caused pain, fear, embarrassment, danger, or other problems. The effectiveness is in heaping fact upon fact with little room for denial by the dependent—but offered in an atmosphere of love and deep concern. Love is the essential element of an intervention—*there is no defense against love.*

Planning for an intervention also involves deciding what treatment or course of action the dependent will be asked to take. When an intervention has been thoroughly planned and everyone has been thoroughly prepared, *most* dependents seek treatment as a result.

However, the intervention members will have decided on the consequences they'll enact if the dependent refuses treatment. Small but concrete consequences are more believable and effective than the threat of major, complex ones. Examples include refusing to ride in a car with the dependent or refusing to socialize or talk with the dependent when he or she has been drinking.

Since alcoholism is a family disease, treatment *must* involve the family. Treatment for the dependent will include detoxification as well as individual and group counseling. Treatment for the family members will include individual and group counseling to break through their own denial and compulsive behaviors. Otherwise the dependent simply returns to the old family system with the old behaviors, and the odds of relapse are extraordinarily high.

During AfterCare, family members begin their work *as a family*. They deal with leftover problems and with new problems that develop as members practice new behaviors. With the completion of AfterCare, the recovering alcoholic and the recovering family members continue their involvement with fellowships such as AA, Al-Anon, Alateen, and community support groups. Recovery becomes a way of living that is based upon staying healthy rather than getting healthy.

But He (or She) Doesn't
Look Like an Alcoholic

Do you picture a homeless person passed out in a back alley under a sheet of newspapers when you hear the word alcoholic? This is true in the extreme, but many, many more alcoholics are "functional" alcoholics.

Functional alcoholics are mothers, fathers, sisters, brothers, aunts, uncles, teachers, ministers, psychiatrists, truck drivers, lawyers, pilots, surgeons, plumbers, bosses, students, and friends.

Functional alcoholics don't necessarily look or act drunk, miss work, drink in the morning or every weekend, become verbally or physically abusive, or have blackouts.

Functional alcoholics do have sleeping problems, sexual problems, family and relationship problems, mood swings, explosions of anger, health problems, financial and legal problems, and spiritual problems.

Functional alcoholics may miss work especially on Monday due to an upset stomach, bad back, sinus headache, allergies, or the "flu." They may want a drink as soon as they get home; need a drink before discussing anything unpleasant; make promises they don't keep; brag about not drinking for a few days, weeks, or months; gulp the first couple of drinks; be uncomfortable where no alcohol is served; or not be able to remember conversations they had when they were drinking.

Functional alcoholics may have convinced family members *they* are the reason the alcoholic is irritable, sarcastic, wants to be alone, skips meals, has mood swings, gets depressed, is forgetful, has money troubles, procrastinates, or won't do things around the house or with the family.

Alcoholism Always Gives Warning Signs But Sometimes No One Listens

1. Have you ever excused your drinking?
2. Have you ever been embarrassed by your drinking?
3. Do you think the best part of the party is the drinking?
4. Do you have to drink to feel good?
5. Do you drink to deal with problems or stress?
6. Have you ever had a loss of memory as a result of drinking?
7. Have you ever driven under the influence?
8. Do you sneak alcohol, either at home or at a party?
9. Do you ever drink alone?
10. Have you ever felt anxious or guilty about your drinking?
11. Have you ever lied to hide your drinking?
12. Do you have a lot of friends who are heavy drinkers?
13. Do you get angry when someone tries to discuss your drinking?
14. Do you have problems caused directly or indirectly by your drinking?
15. Have you ever wondered if you're an alcoholic?

Although one *yes* doesn't mean you're alcoholic, it's still a warning to think about the role alcohol plays in your life. If you answered *yes* to several questions, it's time to do more than think about it. It's time to talk to someone about your drinking. Do it today. *Please.*

Someone I Know Drinks Too Much
What Should I Do?

DON'T

1. Don't accept a lie as the truth. This only encourages the process of denial.

2. Don't accept promises. Do expect agreements to be kept.

3. Don't lose your temper. You lose your effectiveness.

4. Don't do for problem drinkers what they need to do for themselves.

5. Don't let yourself be used or exploited.

6. Don't lecture, scold, praise, blame, threaten, argue, or use the "if you loved me" approach.

7. Don't empty bottles, hide bottles, mark bottles, or drink with the problem drinker.

8. Don't regard this as a family disgrace. It's a family disease.

DO

1. Do openly and honestly face facts.

2. Do accept alcoholism as a treatable disease.

3. Do discover the sources of treatment in your area.

4. Do learn about the diseases of alcoholism and codependency

5. Do encourage the problem drinker to seek treatment.

6. Do seek treatment as a family member.

7. Do remember that recovery takes time and patience.

8. Do offer understanding, support, and love in sobriety.

Adolescent Alcoholism

The National Institute on Alcohol Abuse and Alcoholism estimates there are 3 million teenage alcoholics in this country and several million more who have a serious drinking problem.

Do you know any of them? Here are the four stages to adolescent alcoholism:

Experimental Use:

Adolescents begin their use out of curiosity, sometimes out of a desire to rebel against parents and society, and almost always in the company of friends. It's usually unplanned and is always dependent upon one of the group being able to "get something." The thrill of the sophisticated and illegal is often part of the high, and because there's still low tolerance, the high is easy to achieve.

Regular Use:

With regular use comes higher tolerance. More money is involved, and false IDs solve the problem of supply. Beer remains the most common teen drink. Hangovers are part of the scene, but there's growing pride in being able to handle it. Blackouts are a joke: *"Hey, did I do anything weird last night? I don't remember."* Trouble with parents builds, with lying becoming commonplace. Non-drinking friends, even those from early childhood, are dropped with new drinking friends taking their place. These new friends are never introduced to parents.

Daily Preoccupation:

Drinking occurs several times a week now, with increased solitary and daytime drinking. School activities are dropped, and grades and attendance have dropped dramatically. A steady supply is kept available and hidden. Trouble with parents and school authority figures increases due to truancies and discipline problems. Trouble with law enforcement increases due to legal problems, such as minor consumption or driving under the influence. Adolescents often find themselves on probation about this time.

Dependency:

The adolescent drinks daily now, sometimes in the morning and frequently at lunch with afternoon classes being missed. There is disorientation and confusion about what is normal since being under the influence has become normal. Feelings of guilt and self-hate increase, with thoughts of suicide often increasing. Most classes have been dropped, jobs have been lost, relationships have been damaged or destroyed—but the problem continues. There is now loss of control. Alcohol is the main focus of life.

The Excuses and the Realities
of Adolescent Alcoholism

But I'm a teenager.

So are 3 million other teenage alcoholics.

But I only drink beer.

You get the same amount of alcohol in a 12 ounce can of beer, a 4 ounce glass of wine, or a 1 ounce shot of whiskey. The only difference is how often you go to the bathroom.

But I never get really drunk.

High tolerance is a symptom of chemical dependency.

But I drink only on weekends.

You don't have to drink constantly to drink as an alcoholic.

But I never have blackouts.

Blackouts are one of the symptoms of developing dependency, but not every alcoholic has them.

But I could quit anytime.

You could quit a hundred times. The only time that counts is the last time you quit.

But everyone else does it.

Do they?

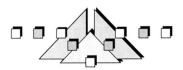

Chapter 10

Children of Alcoholics

Children Without a Childhood

The National Clearinghouse for Alcohol and Drug Information estimates there are 28 million children of alcoholics in this country, with 11 million aged 18 or younger. Children of alcoholics are four times more likely to become alcoholic, and they tend to marry someone *who is* or *will become* alcoholic. Children of alcoholics frequently are victims of incest, neglect, and other forms of abuse.

Children of alcoholics experience overwhelming feelings. They suffer tremendous anxiety, living with the fear that the alcoholic parent will become sick or injured. They also live with fear of the fighting and violence that often erupt between their parents. They learn to expect erratic behavior and frequent crises. Later in life many children of alcoholics live with a need to control every situation because of their continuing fear that something terrible will happen.

Children of alcoholics experience the burdens of guilt, embarrassment, and loneliness. Because no one talks about what's happening in the family, children of alcoholics assume they're to blame. They're afraid to ask anyone for help because they're afraid it's their fault. Since they never know when the crying and shouting will start, they learn not to invite friends to their house. Children of alcoholics quickly become isolated from other children their age.

Children of alcoholics experience confusion. They never know which side of the alcoholic they'll see at the end of the day. Will it be the mom or dad who smiles, laughs, hugs, and plays, or the screaming parent who drags them into the bedroom because they left a sock on the floor? Children of alcoholics also experience role reversal, with the child becoming the parent and the parent becoming the child. They find themselves thrust into the role of caring for their younger siblings and worrying about their parents. They become children without a childhood.

Children of alcoholics experience anger and depression. Their anger, though mostly unexpressed, is at the alcoholic parent for the drinking and at the nonalcoholic parent for the lack of support and protection. Their depression comes from the painful aloneness and from their helplessness to change the situation.

Then the lying starts. Children of alcoholics overhear the nonalcoholic parent lying to the boss, to family members, and to the neighbors. The children's lies start as lies of protection also. Soon children of alcoholics lie most of the time. The lying becomes so compulsive that children of alcoholics lie when it would be just as easy to tell the truth.

These children suffer deep emotional scars. They may be traumatized by being left alone all night, or by having to hide food so they'll have something to eat, or by being physically ill and not having anyone sober enough to notice. This causes what is called "psychic numbing." Children of alcoholics create an artificial emotional distance between what happens to them and how they feel. This becomes a shield from the pain of their emotions, but it also becomes a habitual response to people and situations.

Children of alcoholics desperately need to talk, but they face huge internal struggles. Besides having learned never to trust, they also have been warned never to reveal the family's secret. Add to this their personal sense of shame and guilt together with the emotional distance they create, and it's easy to understand their fear of confiding and their difficulty in expressing their feelings.

The first and most difficult step toward recovery comes when the wall of silence and denial is finally broken. Support groups for children of alcoholics are most effective for this. These groups reduce the children's feelings of isolation, shame, and guilt. There they meet other children who have lived through similar experiences and who share similar feelings. It may be the first time they realize it wasn't because something was *wrong with them*. It also may be the first time they understand that they're not alone.

Children of alcoholics need to understand the *disease* of alcoholism in order to understand their alcoholic parent's behavior. They need to know that their parent is not a bad person; he or she has a disease that causes loss of control when drinking. They need to realize that their responses and the roles they adopted were normal ones for an abnormal situation. They need to express the long suppressed feelings of shame, guilt, confusion, anger, and terror. They need to reconstruct the past from their new perspective and awareness. They need to develop a sense of themselves as individuals, rather than as extensions of an alcoholic. They need to have fun and to develop positive, nurturing relationships. Children of alcoholics need to know that while their past is a part of them, the future is theirs.

The message children of alcoholics have lived with is:

> Don't talk.

> Don't feel.

> Don't trust.

> Don't question.

The message they need to hear is:

> You didn't cause it.

> You can't control it.

> You can't cure it.

> But you can cope with it

>> because you're not alone.

Indications That a Child
May Be Living With Family Alcoholism

1. Frequent tardiness, especially on Monday mornings
2. Anxiety over getting home promptly at the end of the day
3. Being dressed improperly for the weather
4. Poor physical hygiene
5. Extreme maturity or immaturity
6. Avoidance of conflict or extreme argumentativeness
7. Isolation
8. Poor attendance or school failure
9. Physical complaints, especially head and stomach aches
10. Fatigue and listlessness
11. Hyperactivity and difficulty concentrating
12. Emotional outbursts
13. Exaggerated concern with achievement
14. Extreme fear about situations involving contact with parents
15. Extreme negativism about alcohol
16. Unusual attention to alcohol in situations where it's not the focus
17. Lingering by the teacher
18. Mention of a parent's drinking to excess
19. Mention of a friend who has a parent with a drinking problem
20. Concern about whether alcoholism is inherited

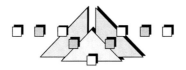

Chapter 11

Grief

"Mourn with those who mourn,
and rejoice with those who rejoice."

Life is a procession of love and loss, joy and pain. Those who love greatly in life are also those who grieve deeply in loss. Walls erected to keep the pain out also keep the love out. To live life fully, we must live with loss.

Our losses range from disappointment to devastation. Some losses we assimilate in a few weeks or months: We try out for a team and are turned down. A girlfriend or boyfriend rejects us. A good friend moves to another city. Other losses may take years to reconcile: We develop a debilitating disease. Our marriage ends in divorce. We lose a loved one to death. Grief becomes the price of living and loving.

To heal a loss, we must *grieve*. We cannot avoid it; we can only delay it. When we deny feelings of grief, we manage only to lengthen the process and to delay our healing. The feelings of loss will surface at some later time but in more complex and confusing ways.

The length of time people need to grieve is different for each person. It depends on the importance of the event in their life. It depends on the frequency and timing of other losses they've suffered. It depends on the support and understanding they receive. It depends on how *actively* they grieve their loss.

People also must grieve in their own individual ways. Some people cry continuously for days while others may not cry for weeks or months or years. Some people make changes in their lives while others keep everything exactly the same. The important thing is that people be allowed to grieve in the way they need.

While the pain is most intense for the first six to eight weeks, the worst time often comes after anyone thinks support is needed. By the time the shock wears off, grieving people may find that no one will talk about it anymore, saying they need to quit dwelling on it. People do this unconsciously to protect their *own* feelings, and they end up withdrawing support when it's still needed. They do this because they can no longer bear to see their friend in pain and feel there is nothing they can do.

Yet, there is a great deal we can do as friends. Listening is the greatest gift we can offer. This is especially true when the *way* we listen gives people permission to be genuine. When we accept where *they* are, we make no further demands on them. Grieving people frequently need to tell the same stories over and over again. It helps when a friend understands that they're going to need to tell these stories until they *don't need* to tell them any more.

The hardest part is that we want to take away the pain. But there's no way to fix this or make it better, and words often will fail us. Then just holding each other and crying helps more than anything to take away the loneliness and pain. Grief heals best when it's shared with others. As a friend what we offer is not doing *for* them but being *with* them.

Elisabeth Kübler-Ross (1975) has identified the five stages of grief listed below. People don't necessarily go through each stage or go through them in order, and they often will work through various stages only to go back to them over and over.

The first stage is *denial.* The immediate reaction is, *"No! There must be some mistake."* This initial reaction of denial and disbelief is the body's psychological shock absorber. People often will go on "automatic pilot," seeming to function normally but with a numbing *"this can't be happening"* sensation. The denial and numbness are defense mechanisms and need to be treated gently.

The second stage is *anger*. When denial fades, the anger comes. *"Why me?"* or *"Why him?"* The anger comes from feelings of pain, abandonment, helplessness, and fear. People sometimes will lash out or blame others in their pain. Healthy options for ventilating anger are to scream into a pillow, pound on a sofa or mattress, rip up a stack of newspapers, or throw ice cubes against a brick wall.

The third stage is *bargaining*. Bargaining comes in the form of the if only's: *"If only we hadn't had that argument."* *"If only I had kept him here five more minutes."* *"If only I had said I love you."* Or, it may come as an attempt to bargain with God: *"If only You'll let her live, I'll donate the rest of my life to helping people."*

The fourth stage is *depression*. As reality sets in, the sense of loss deepens. Saying good-bye to someone or to life begins here. The depression is a reaction to a changed way of life caused by loss—loss of love and loss of hope.

The fifth stage is *acceptance.* This is best described as reconciliation or assimilation, rather than recovery. We never totally get over a deep loss. Instead we become reconciled and learn to assimilate it into the new reality of our life. Finally the day comes when we awaken ready to get on with life, while knowing we'll never forget. For the dying person this is a time of peaceful, quiet acceptance.

Grief is frequently complicated by guilt. It's not unusual for adults and children alike to blame themselves after a death or to feel guilty for things said or unsaid. Young children are particularly vulnerable because of their "magical thinking." They believe that thinking something makes it happen. Since most children have wished at least once that their parents would go away and leave them alone, a child may suffer in silence for years if a parent dies.

Memories are difficult at first, causing some of our most vivid and painful feelings. Later these same memories give comfort because they keep a person with us. It sometimes helps to gently remind people that their loved one wouldn't want to see them continue to hurt. They would want them getting on with the lessons of life—living, learning, loving.

Grief Care

For Yourself

- Go gently. Don't push. Your body needs rest, nutrition, and time to repair.
- Ask for help when you need it and accept help when it's offered.
- Keep decision making to a minimum.
- Accept the pain. You can't outrun it. Fully enter the grieving process.
- Keep a journal. It will help you understand what you're feeling.
- Let yourself cry. It's a natural and necessary part of healing.
- Exercise. It will help you work off frustration and sleep better.
- Read some good books on grief. Understanding grief helps you handle it.
- Invite a friend or relative for dinner or overnight.
- It's okay to be angry. Let it out. Hit a pillow. Yell. Go for a walk. Talk about it.
- Give yourself something to look forward to each day.
- Do something for someone else. Helping takes our mind off ourselves.
- Plan new interests. Join a group. Rediscover old interests, friends, or activities.
- If holidays or certain days are hard, plan something comforting.
- Don't feel guilty when you have a good time. It's what we want for you.
- Bring balance to your life: pray, work, play, and rest.

For Others

- Invite your friend to tell you where he or she was when he or she heard the news, what happened next, what is happening now.
- Ask to see a picture. Encourage your friend to tell you stories and share memories.
- Find out if your friend has been having bad dreams. Listen.
- Help your friend write a letter to say the things he or she left unsaid or to say good-bye.
- Listen for signs of survivor guilt: *"I should have died instead of him."*

  Or relief guilt: *"I'm actually relieved. She suffered so long."*

  Or joy guilt: *"I could never feel happy again."*
- Make a collage of words and pictures that reminds your friend of his or her loved one and the times they shared.
- Help your friend write a letter to an estranged relative or friend.
- Offer concrete assistance. Offer to help with a report, to run an errand, to go with your friend to talk with someone.
- Send cards or goofy notes and call unexpectedly to check on your friend.
- Remind your friend that there are no shortcuts. Healing takes time.
- Be available.

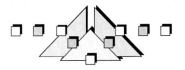

Chapter 12

Rape

The word rape evokes the image of a hooded stranger lurking in a dimly lit parking lot or alley waiting for his victim to appear. Although rape occurs in these situations, the chilling fact is that rape also is committed in homes, on weekend outings, and by people who are the victim's acquaintances, friends, and dates.

It is estimated that over:

- Half of all of all rapes are by someone the victim knows.
- Half of all of all rapes are in the daytime.
- Half of all of all rapes are in the victim's or attacker's home.

The grim reality is that over half of all rapes occur with people, at times, and in places where the victim doesn't expect to be in danger. It's estimated that one in four girls and one in six boys are sexually molested by the age of 18. Although the rape victim will be referred to as female here, it's important to recognize that boys and men also are raped. This event often is even more destructive and devastating for them because of societal views.

Rape is not a crime of passion. Studies have shown that most rapists have active sexual relationships and that most rapes are premeditated. Rape is a crime of power and violence in which the weapon is sex and the intent is to degrade and humiliate another human being.

Most rape victims react first to the terror of being raped and later to the sexual aspects of the crime. If the important people around her, particularly her male friends and family members, become obsessed by the sexual nature of the crime, it only increases and complicates the guilt, confusion, and devastation she feels. Since she's *already* overwhelmed, she's particularly vulnerable to the reactions of those around her.

A deep feeling of guilt is her strongest and most common reaction. She continuously asks herself what it is about *her* that caused her to be raped, and this explains a great deal about the small percentage of rapes that are reported. While the embarrassment and humiliation are factors, it's the sense of *being responsible* that holds women back. Women need to understand that a person intent on raping chooses a victim because she's available, rather than for anything particular about her.

The woman's health needs must be dealt with as soon as possible. She needs to be checked for internal and external injuries, sexually transmitted diseases, and pregnancy. Hospital emergency rooms are best equipped to do the necessary tests. The woman shouldn't shower or change clothes before receiving medical attention in order to preserve evidence.

A rape victim is encouraged at least to report the incident since this doesn't commit her to further legal action. Most rapists are repeat offenders, and her report may be the one that puts a stop to the crimes. If she's filed a report, she has the option to decide later whether or not to prosecute.

A woman will have many strong emotional needs which also must be met as soon as possible. A warm, concerned, and loving response from her family and friends probably does more to help than anything else. She needs to feel believed, accepted, and loved. While it's important for her to talk about the assault, it needs to be as general or specific as she chooses and *only* when she's ready.

The rape victim goes through all the stages of grief: denial, anger, bargaining, depression, and assimilation. The stage of depression is when she actually begins to face the reality of the rape, and it can be the hardest stage. Professional help can be extremely beneficial at this stage or at any time.

A rape victim will be left with many issues. Guilt is ongoing, and a woman needs to be reminded that she was not responsible for the rape. She needs to understand that feeling guilty is not the same as being guilty. Her thinking needs to be challenged gently but firmly: *"If you blame yourself, then do you blame other rape victims?"* and *"Would you blame yourself if you had been robbed?"*

Trust becomes a major issue for rape victims. They often go from one extreme to the other, from trusting everyone to trusting no one. While being cautious and aware definitely increase her safety, a woman needs to be reminded that there are people she can trust. She needs reassurance that as her confidence in her judgment returns, she'll have an increasing ability to decide whom to trust.

The feelings of fear and vulnerability are overwhelming at times, and rape victims experience flashbacks and nightmares. However, what she doesn't need is to feel helpless. Fathers, husbands, and boyfriends sometimes will refuse to let her go anywhere alone. This only increases her sense of weakness, and it may increase her sense of guilt as well. A course in self-defense or assertiveness training will be empowering for her.

Problems with male relationships are predictable and understandable at first. A woman may feel sordid, dirty, or ruined. She needs to affirm her positive qualities as a person and her contributions as a human being, apart from her sexuality. She may have difficulty with intimacy for a time, but these feelings usually pass with an understanding partner.

Being unable to express anger is a sign of depression, with the anger turned inward. When feelings of anger begin to surface, it's a *good sign* of beginning recovery. A rape victim needs to be encouraged and supported in her expressions of anger. She needs to write and talk about her fears, nightmares, and feelings. She needs to increase her physical outlets as another way to vent her anger. For some women, prosecuting the rapist is what allows them finally to let go of their anger.

As devastating as it is, sexual assault is not so devastating that a person cannot recover. When people have the loving support of family and friends and are able to talk about their fears and feelings, a stronger person will emerge. Many women have found that helping others deal with similar experiences is what helped them finally to assimilate the event and to regain a sense of control in their lives.

Date Rape

Date rape is an increasingly common crime in our society, particularly in school settings. Because date rape occurs within relationship—whether new or longstanding—it's a crime that often is misunderstood by both men and women. Yet, date rape is a violent crime that carries serious consequences for both people.

As a woman you must

- Speak clearly about your limits.
- Don't give mixed messages. A man cannot read your mind.
- Understand that drugs and alcohol are a factor in most cases.
- Trust your instincts. Leave if a person or place makes you uneasy.
- Know the person you're going out with or go with a group.
- Never leave a party or game with someone you don't know well.
- Watch for characteristics that can signal trouble:

  A man who belittles you,
  ignores your thoughts and feelings,
  shows aggressive behaviors,
  talks badly about previous girlfriends,
  is extremely jealous, or
  takes offense when you disagree.

As a man you must

- Listen carefully. If you get mixed messages, ask.
- Avoid the myth that a woman means yes when she says no. No means no. Respect her answer.
- Don't let your judgment be clouded by drugs or alcohol.
- Don't make assumptions based on style of dress, behavior, or setting.
- Be especially careful in groups and resist any pressure to participate in violent or criminal acts.
- Know that it is never acceptable to use force or coercion in sexual relationships, no matter the circumstances.
- Realize that sex with someone who is mentally or physically incapable of giving consent is rape.
- Get involved if you see someone who is at risk.
- Speak out. Your sister or future girlfriend could be affected.

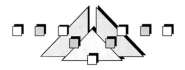

Chapter 13

Your Family, Yourself

Your family experience is one of the most significant influences in your life, determining much of who you are, who you become, what you value, and what you believe. From your family you either learn or don't learn how to love, laugh, cry, play, work, share, earn, communicate, and appreciate.

Many find that the lessons they learned from family serve them well, and they continue to build upon them. Others find the opposite to be true. Their work involves first unlearning old lessons before replacing them with new ones. Either way you learn from your family. You learn either how you want to be or how you don't want to be. Your family begins the process. Where you go from there is up to you.

Few groups will ever test you like your family. It's one thing to get along with your friends, your teachers, or your boss. It's an entirely different matter to get along with family—sharing chores, bedrooms, bathrooms, growing room. Tension and conflict are inevitable.

There never will be another group that you *should* on like your family. Teens in particular tend to think that their family should be what they would like them to be. They *should* be cool. They *should* know more things. They *should* be like the family down the street.

This attitude ignores a significant fact about your family. Your parents learned to be parents from their parents. It's the family model they have, consciously or unconsciously. This is the case whether your parents were happy or unhappy as children. You can learn important information about your parents and family by looking closely at their relationship with *their* parents.

However, parents need to remember that children *will* make mistakes and that making mistakes and experiencing their consequences is part of growing up. It's essential that a child's worth in the family not be linked to his or her success. Then the family becomes the support system it's *designed to be* in helping the children pick themselves up, dust off their feelings of failure, and get on with it.

If there *is* a secret to building a happy family, it begins with parents and children alike treating each other the way they treat their friends and those they value. Some families could begin by treating each other with the courtesy given to a perfect stranger. While this doesn't *solve* the problems of family, it prevents many new ones from being created. It also creates an environment in which family members *want* to see problems solved.

With your friends, you trust and are trustworthy. With your friends, you forgive and are forgiven. With your friends, you are patient, kind, and accepting. You are available and supportive. You are respectful. You *communicate* with your friends. When you will treat your family as you do your friends, your family will become your friends—sometimes your best friends.

One of the challenges every family faces is compromise. Of course there are the *non-negotiables* parents must set such as no alcohol or drugs, no broken curfews, no reckless driving, and so on. With these exceptions, one of the most powerful ways parents can acknowledge their children is to compromise with them. To compromise demonstrates respect for their concerns while validating their importance as people. Compromise teaches a significant life lesson, the settling of differences by mutual concession and respect.

No family can become happier and healthier by focusing on the negative. You may be painfully aware of what you don't like about your family. But have you taken the time to acknowledge and appreciate the sacrifices and provisions made for you? Instead of what you wish your family would stop doing, what do you hope they always will keep doing?

Focusing on the positive leads to more that is positive. A family that laughs together and has fun creates a balance for the stresses that *will* occur. A family that shares feelings and needs is equipped to express appreciation and affection as well as needed improvement. A family that accepts and loves each other *as they are* will grow into what they can become.

You can improve your family by becoming a better family member. Begin with this question: *"What can I do to make this family one to treasure?"*

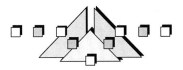

Chapter 14

Divorce

Disintegration of a Family

In the last 50 or more years the American family has undergone vast changes:

Then:

Most families were part of a rural, farming community. Many people lived in the same community—and the same house—all their lives. People built their own houses, grew their own food, and work was something that was done at home.

Now:

Most families are part of an urban community. Most people leave home to go to work, trading skills for money to purchase food and shelter.

Then:

Marriage was an economic necessity for both men and women. A man needed a wife to prepare and preserve food while he worked in the fields; he needed a wife to bear and raise the children who would someday help him. A woman needed a husband to support and protect her.

Now:

Marriage is an emotional rather than an economic decision. It's a decision made from a desire for happiness rather than from necessity. People now wait longer to marry and are more likely to end a marriage if they're not happy.

Then:

Divorce was highly unusual. Marriage was understood as a sacred covenant, and partners stayed together for better or for worse. Divorce wasn't economically possible for most women. Society strongly disapproved, and the stigma of divorce made it difficult for divorced men and women to be accepted in society.

Now:

Divorce is commonplace and readily accepted by society. It is predicted that as many as half of all recent marriages will end in divorce.

Then:

The only single parents were widows or widowers. Death was the only thing that dissolved families, and the widow or widower usually quickly remarried.

Now:

Single parent families are rapidly increasing with nearly a third of all children under the age of 18 living in single parent households.

According to the U.S. Bureau of the Census, the number of divorced people has more than tripled in the last thirty years. However, the fact that divorce is common does not prevent or minimize the pain for those involved, especially for the children.

There are several factors that determine how children will cope with divorce. The environment in which they lived *before the divorce* has a profound effect. If the environment was one of open conflict, the children already will have developed coping problems. On the other hand if the marriage partners simply had given up on the relationship, there may have been the illusion of peace. This also creates great difficulty and confusion for the children.

Another factor for children is how the divorce is announced. If the announcement is made with no preparation by the parents, the children experience increased fear and anxiety. A decision to divorce needs to be communicated by both parents with the entire family together, but *only* after the parents have anticipated the needs and questions of the children. Information is much easier for children to deal with than what their imaginations will create.

Although children experience different needs at different ages, some needs are constant with *all age groups*. Children need to understand that no one parent is solely responsible for the divorce. They need to believe in the worth of both parents and to maintain a consistent, loving relationship with each. They need to know that even though their parents have decided to divorce, their love for the children will last forever. They need never to be used as pawns in a battle between their parents. They need to be allowed to stay in familiar surroundings, attending the same school with the same friends. They need to be told that they are not responsible for the divorce. They need to mourn the loss of their parents as a couple, and they need to grieve at their own pace.

Their age and developmental stage are important factors in how children respond initially. How well they understand what is happening helps determine how well they assimilate the experience. In general younger children have a more difficult time than older ones.

Here are the responses and corresponding needs of children based on their developmental stages:

Preschool (3-5):

These children are frightened, confused, and experiencing anxiety. They often deny the reality of the divorce as a way to deal with it. They frequently develop eating and sleeping disturbances and may regress to earlier, more immature behaviors such as thumb sucking or clinging. They show a general fearfulness, but they have particularly strong fears of punishment and rejection, imagining that they will be sent away or replaced. They tend to feel guilty and to blame themselves for the divorce, and this sometimes manifests in the "too-good child."

This age group needs strong reassurance that they will be cared for and loved. They need increased physical contact and comfort, and they need consistency in daily routines and discipline. They may need to hear repeated explanations of what the arrangements will be and what the divorce will mean. They will need help in understanding the connection between the divorce and what they're experiencing, such as feelings of sadness, nightmares, and so on.

Early School Age (6-8):

These children experience deep feelings of sadness and grief, though they are less likely to feel guilty for the divorce. They feel confused, helpless, betrayed, deprived, and rejected. They experience strong feelings of anger but difficulty expressing it. These children are torn by strong loyalty conflicts, and they suffer deep insecurity, fearing the loss of the custodial parent as well. They have an intense desire for reconciliation, and they fantasize that the absent parent will walk in one day and the family will be together again. They are old enough to understand what is happening without being old enough to cope effectively.

This age group needs help in expressing their feelings and putting them in perspective. They need structure and consistency. Their reconciliation fantasy needs to be acknowledged while they are led gently to accept the finality of the divorce. They need to know that they can love and enjoy both parents without worry of hurting the other one. They need free and easy access to both parents and regular contact with the noncustodial parent.

Older School Age (9-12):

These children experience intense anger, feeling outraged at having to "lose" one of their parents. Because they see things in black and white terms, they often will blame and reject one parent. They may become demanding, using temper tantrums and guilt to get what they want. They frequently choose tough or indifferent exteriors to cover their feelings of insecurity and vulnerability. They experience deep feelings of loneliness and rejection, resentment and shame. They are sensitive and prone to worry, often becoming overinvolved with the custodial parent.

This age group needs their anger recognized and their manipulation exposed, openly but lovingly. They need to enjoy a realistic appreciation of both parents because this enhances their own feelings of worth. They need to be secure in daily arrangements and to have continuity and consistency with both parents. They fear betraying one parent by talking to the other, so they can benefit from talking to someone outside the family.

Adolescence (13-18):

These young people experience deep feelings of sadness, loss, betrayal, and anger. They sometimes act out their feelings through increased use of alcohol or other drugs, promiscuity, or delinquency. They frequently are resentful at having to deal with yet another burden during a time when they already feel burdened by life. They worry about the implications of their parents' divorce on their own future marriage. They are concerned about money and the family's finances. They often adopt a pseudo-maturity, becoming independent at a much earlier age.

This age group needs to express their feelings and fears directly and to understand they are not extensions of their parents. They frequently need to disengage from events and get on with their own lives. They need to be kept appropriately informed but never used as a confidant by one or both parents. Although they will need to take more responsibility, they are *not* the absent parent and cannot be responsible for adults. They need guidance and boundaries, and they need parents who are parents, not pals.

Divorce is a complex and ongoing process that involves more than just the divorce itself. The degree of parental conflict has more effect on the children than whether the parents are married or divorced. Even after a divorce, how the parents relate determines the quality of other family relationships. If the family must move because of finances, this becomes an additional factor in the children's ability to adjust.

While the difficulties for children in dealing with divorce cannot be overstated, children *can* cope successfully and *will* emerge as stronger people when their needs are met. The new opportunities for growth may enrich their lives when they love and are loved by every member of their family.

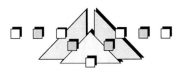

Chapter 15

Stepfamilies

Learning to Walk in Step

The profile of the American family has changed dramatically in the last few decades. Although we still have the traditional family consisting of father, mother, and approximately two children, these families are no longer the norm. We now have growing numbers of single parent families together with an increasing number of families in which grandparents do the parenting. Also in ever increasing numbers are our stepfamilies consisting of father/stepfather, mother/stepmother, and children/stepchildren.

Although some stepfamilies occur due to the death of one of the parents, most of our stepfamilies today are formed as a result of divorce. Most divorced people remarry and about half of the remarriages involve children.

Stepfamilies are different from biological families. The most significant difference is that the stepfamily is born of loss. It comes into existence due to a personal loss by every member of the stepfamily. The children will have "lost" a parent. At least one of the stepparents will have lost a partner. Even a previously unmarried stepparent will have lost the dream of a traditional family. Every person is in some stage of grief.

Because people grieve at different rates, a remarriage sometimes occurs before the children have resolved their grief and are ready to be part of a new family. These children experience a double failure—failure to hold the first marriage together and failure to keep the second one apart.

While the parent and stepparent also are dealing with loss, they frequently grieve for a shorter time than the children, especially when they wanted the end of the marriage. Adults who are part of a stepfamily have chosen this way of life, but children become part of a stepfamily through no choice of their own. A remarriage can become yet another loss to be absorbed.

Many stepfamilies come together with an expectation of "instant love" between the children, stepparents, and step-siblings. Stepparents often experience guilt, frustration, and rejection when this doesn't happen, not realizing they're trying to achieve an impossible goal. Love takes time, and it's enough at first if stepfamily members respect and enjoy each other. Any further demands for affection only create additional pressure.

Each person brings a different history and belief system to the stepfamily. In order to blend two major ways of doing things, the stepfamily must develop creative new approaches from old traditions. This includes everything from how holidays are celebrated—*"We open our gifts on Christmas morning."* *"Well, we open ours on Christmas Eve"*—to how family members relate. The new stepfamily will have to decide who does which chores and on what schedule. They'll have to decide whether children earn their spending money or are given an allowance. They'll have to decide whether people clean their plate or eat what they want, whether they work first or play first, which television shows they watch, and so on. One of the most difficult new questions is who disciplines whom, how, and for what.

Resolving these questions is complicated by the fact that the children frequently are members of more than one household. There is usually a biological parent to be taken into consideration. The stepfamily members who are present at any given time change because of custody and visitation arrangements. The boundaries of the new family are blurred.

Stepfamilies also experience more "triangles" than biological families. The child/parent relationship is of longer duration than the parent/stepparent relationship. There is an emotional and legal bond between the child/parent and between the parent/stepparent, but there is no legal and often no emotional bond between the child/stepparent and child/stepsiblings.

Children in stepfamilies often experience changes in their family position such as going from being the oldest child to the youngest. A child also can go from being the only girl or boy in the family to being one of several. Children find themselves sharing space and possessions with new stepsiblings.

Probably the most accurate single word description of stepfamilies is *complex.* Many don't realize that the problems they encounter are due to the complexities and uncertainties of their family system.

Stepfamily members need to participate in negotiating and establishing new traditions. Regular family meetings provide a structure for developing positive solutions. There stepfamily members learn how to express their loss and needs appropriately. Family meetings are used for encouraging, planning, praying, sharing, grieving, and celebrating. Old loyalties are cherished and maintained while new alliances and friendships are forged.

Although stepfamilies tend to be more stressful than intact, biological families, many find a special satisfaction and sense of accomplishment in their stepfamilies. Stepfamilies are more aware of the precious and fragile nature of relationships, working harder to maintain them. There is a deep sense of joy in being part of a family that was conceived in loss and matured in personal gain for each family member.

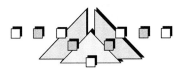

Chapter 16

Stress Mastery

Modern life is full of stress, but some stress is *good* for us. Stress provides the edge that makes life exciting and challenging. Stress is what motivates us to do our best, to try new things, to achieve our goals. The challenge with stress is not in learning to eliminate it but in learning to master it.

When you're under stress, your body responds with a surge of adrenaline and other hormones, your heart beats faster, respiration speeds up, muscles tense, blood pressure and blood sugar rise, perspiration increases, and digestion stops. These responses prepare you for sudden action, for "fight or flight."

This is all good if your source of stress is a car speeding at you in the crosswalk. However, if your source of stress is a pop quiz or an argument with your parents, your body has to return to normal without burning off the excess energy in physical reaction. Regular repetition of the stress response and readjustment cycle can damage your body, eventually exhausting your ability to bounce back.

Dr. Robert Sharpe and David Lewis (1977) describe stress as the "fire of life." People tend to feel about stress the way primitive people felt about fire. They couldn't control it, and they saw the destruction and pain it caused. But fire also gives light and warmth when we learn to contain it. Stress, like fire, can bring destruction and misery or creativity and energy to our life.

Different things are more, or less, stressful for different people. Our level of stress is a result of our skill or preparation in a situation. Being attacked by a mugger is more stressful for a little old lady than for a little old lady with a black belt in karate.

Stress is everything in our environment that places a demand upon us. However, it's our *perception* that determines our response. If you awaken on a Saturday morning and the clock reads 10:00 a.m., you may delight in the thought of a lazy day. However, if you were due at work at 9:00 a.m., your perception will be entirely different. Stress is neutral. It's our reaction that gives it the positive or negative influence in our life.

The story of the two frogs that fell into a bucket of cream demonstrates this. The first frog was a tried and true pessimist, and he just knew it was hopeless. So he flung up his little flipper feet and drowned. The second frog was a real fighter, and he just knew there had to be a way out. So he swam and swam and swam and, lo and behold, his kicking churned the cream into butter. He folded his little frog legs and making one bold leap, hopped merrily away.

Even though both frogs were *totally stressed,* they dealt with it in completely different ways. We often discover our solutions through positive attitude, single-minded purpose, and focused effort.

Stress that is experienced as upsetting or destructive is called distress. Stress that is experienced as motivating or useful is called *eustress,* from the Greek word for good. However, our physical reaction to both forms of stress is similar. The line between the eustress that turns you on and the distress that wears you out is a fine one.

Each of us needs different levels of stress, and these levels vary from day to day and from situation to situation. What we strive for is what Sharpe and Lewis call our optimum stress level, the level of stress at which we work most successfully with no mental or physical ill effects.

If the level of stress falls *below* our optimum stress level, our performance will be impaired from boredom, lack of enthusiasm, and difficulty concentrating. If the level of stress rises *above* our optimum stress level, our performance will be impaired from anxiety, tension, and difficulty concentrating.

The goal is to find the level that's right for you. You're like a guitar. Each of the strings of a guitar is different and is strung under a different level of tension. The A string requires a certain tension level to function while the E string requires a different level. Tighten them too much and they snap. Relax them too much and they don't make music.

So we know what stress is, how it affects us, and what it does for us. But *how* do we control it? Here is a decision-making approach, called the 3 A's of Stress Mastery. This method is adapted from the work of Joe E. Dunlap and J. Douglas Stewart (1983) and also Nancy and Donald Tubesing (1983).

The 3 A's of Stress Mastery are:

- Alter
- Avoid
- Accept

The first A is *alter.* Can you remove the stress by changing something? One change may be to communicate your feelings to someone. When Brian, a high school senior, explained to his mother that his bedroom was one of the few places he felt in charge, she was more inclined to accept his untidy habits.

Or, do you need to change yourself? Stress often is caused by lack of planning or by poor organization and time management. Waiting until the night before a paper is due is a sure way to create stress. Or, back to Brian, when he understood how important the appearance of the house was to his mother, he realized that being neater would remove a chronic source of stress, their disagreements about his room.

The second A is *avoid.* Can you get away from the stress physically? If your job in a busy fast food restaurant makes you irritable all day, continue to search for a job in a setting you enjoy where you're learning skills you value.

If you can't get away physically, you can get away mentally. If there are no other jobs, quit fighting what you can't change. Focus instead on the aspects of the job you *enjoy* such as the wide variety of people you meet or how quickly the time passes. Learn also to suggest alternate ways of doing things.

The third A is *accept*. Sometimes a situation, although stressful, is where you want or need to be. If you can't alter it or avoid it, then you must equip yourself to cope with it.

This is the ABC's of Accepting:

- Acknowledge
- Balance
- Control

The **A** is *acknowledge*. Recognize that it's your choice and your decision to remain in the situation. For now at least, you have more to gain than to lose by remaining where you are. Explain your decision to someone, write it down, and remind yourself often.

The **B** is *balance*. To remain healthy you must provide balance by becoming stronger:

- Physically through nutrition, exercise, and relaxation
- Mentally through positive attitude and focus on priorities and goals
- Socially through supportive relationships and honest communication
- Spiritually through prayer and meditation

The **C** is *control*. It's not what happens to us but what we *think* about what happens to us that determines how we feel. You must control your perception of the situation or of yourself in order to function in a healthy way. You can transform negative feelings by remembering that every person, situation, or relationship is an opportunity to learn about yourself. You can free yourself from fear of failure by focusing on what you will have learned or gained.

So how can *you* put the 3 A's of Stress Mastery into action? What personal situation could you approach differently using this method for stress mastery? *Try it out now....*

What did you discover? Remember that different responses work for different people at different times. The key is finding what works for you, at this time, in this situation.

May all your stress be eustress!

Do You Know Your Stress Symptoms?

Physical

❏ fatigue
❏ digestive problems
❏ headaches
❏ eating changes
❏ lack of energy
❏ profuse sweating
❏ dry mouth
❏ insomnia
❏ susceptibility to colds/flu
❏ accident prone
❏ tense muscles
❏ hives
❏ grinding teeth
❏ pounding heart
❏ restlessness
❏ alcohol, drugs, tobacco
❏ cold hands/feet
❏ other

Emotional

❏ cynical
❏ easily frustrated
❏ lack of direction
❏ nervous laugh
❏ worrying
❏ irritability
❏ temper displays
❏ crying
❏ discouragement
❏ sadness
❏ helplessness
❏ hopelessness
❏ anxiety
❏ nightmares
❏ depression
❏ mood swings
❏ other

Mental

❏ confusion
❏ lack of concentration
❏ forgetting
❏ low productivity
❏ mind going blank
❏ dulled senses
❏ lack of creativity
❏ spacing out
❏ negativity
❏ other

Relational

❏ lashing out
❏ withdrawing
❏ nagging
❏ unforgiving
❏ critical
❏ resentful
❏ lack of intimacy
❏ blaming
❏ comments of family,
   friends, co-workers
❏ other

The 3 A's of Stress Mastery

Describe your situation:

List *alter* responses: Can you change something? Can you change yourself?

List *avoid* responses: Can you get away from the stress physically or mentally?

List *accept* responses: What are your ABC's of Accepting?

Acknowledge:

Balance:

Control:

Which response is the best one for you at this time in this situation?

101 Stress Strategies

• Talk to a friend • Laugh often • Keep a journal • Plant a garden • Have a spare key • Feed the birds • Make a list • Remember you have a choice • Plan ahead • Go for a walk • Develop a support network • Cook a special meal • Listen to classical music • Read a good book • Clean your room • Smile • See the promise in problems • Ask for help • Lift weights • Pet your pet • Fix things when they break • Don't have all the answers • Get up earlier • Do something you've dreamed of • Know your priorities • Play some everyday • Go a new way • Watch the sunset • Eat lots of fruit and vegetables • Meditate on what is good, kind, or lovely • Own your feelings • Roast marshmallows • Ask yourself if it really matters • Compliment someone • Take a break • Avoid power struggles • Pray • Bake cookies • Face your fears • Have something to look forward to • Avoid drugs • Be early for appointments • Breathe deeply • Say no • Embrace your challenges • Take a warm bath • Know your limits • Stop rehearsing and do something • Call an old friend • Do dreaded jobs first • Be gracious • See the funny side of things • Change your routine • Have a "Plan B" • Do something for someone else • Get enough sleep • Take a risk • Sing in the shower • Speak assertively • Listen • Give hugs • Read a story to a child • Work for excellence, forget perfection • Go for a bike ride • Tickle someone • Expect good things • Be grateful • Count to ten • Notice patterns • Decide what you really want • Cut down on salt and sugar • Avoid limited thinking • Go dancing • Maintain your weight • Recognize your uniqueness • Live one day at a time • Don't pretend • Break bread with someone • Honor your values • Remember that people do the best they know how • Be still • Recognize guidance • Learn when to act and when to wait • Forgive • Get a massage • Pay attention • Do what you love • Exercise • See the good • Look for a winning solution • Check agreements • Take small steps • Plan for a rainy day • Empower others • Be open to receive • Surround yourself with positive people • Learn to let go • Keep it simple • Remember that you have all the time there is • Love people • Trust God

Section IV
Support Group Program

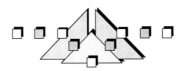

Chapter 17

Group Leadership

The Leading Role

Yours is the leading role. You set the stage and draw the crowd. You give them a peek behind the curtain, a look at the program. This is your show now—but it will be theirs very soon. Nervous excitement is only natural and it fills the room. Everyone feels it. But you're the one who says it: *"I'm nervous. I'm excited. I'm so glad you're here."* These are your opening lines. Your vulnerability makes their vulnerability safer. And the show begins.

The nervous excitement passes quickly. However, if any anxiety in the group is due to fear of rejection, you'll need to be patient to get them past this point. When people feel anxious, they fall back on social behaviors that have worked for them in the past—being cool, being silly, being silent, being superior, being confused. It's not until they trust you that they'll try *being honest* instead.

There is hushed anticipation. Everyone is hoping something special is about to begin. And they want a part to play in it. They will have to share something of themselves to become known to this group. Their early disclosures are tentative, and while there's lots of talking there's not a lot being said. Not yet, anyway.

The shuffling sounds quiet down. A silence falls on the group. However, only one person normally talks at a time. Silence is just a time when one more person than normal is quiet. Silence is a natural—and productive—part of group interaction. Your focus needs to be on the *meaning* of the silence. Is it the silence that happens when people are deciding how to respond? Is it the silence that means people don't understand? Is it the silence that follows a deeply emotional experience? Or, is it the silence that says people are afraid?

Your role is to protect them as they relate to each other. Two important things happen when people risk sharing similar feelings. One is that they discover they're not alone. *"So it's not just me."* The other is that a bond begins to grow and develop within the group. When nurtured, this bond leads to a special closeness in the group called group *cohesion.* If a group doesn't achieve cohesion, the members still will benefit. However, when there is cohesion in a group, it vastly accelerates and deepens growth.

A group is a stage, a platform for growth and change. People are taught in other places to deny feelings: *"Big boys don't cry"* or *"You're such a baby."* When people deny feelings, they deny themselves. Here they interact honestly and openly, with an emphasis on feelings. They reconstruct their past from a new perspective and with a new awareness of their individuality. They observe different ways of being and behaving. They learn how they are perceived—and how they see themselves.

Here people *give* as well as receive help. People often will say to others what they really need to say to themselves. *"David, I don't like it when you put yourself down. You're too critical."* Groups are great at spotting connections like this. *"And so are you!"* In giving support, the group members receive support and a challenge to a higher way of being.

The bonds within the group continue to deepen, and the group members display an increasing concern for each other. Individual differences are appreciated for the opportunities they provide the group. Their new insight is opening doors to a deeper understanding of each other—and themselves.

The group members practice new roles and ways of relating in the group. As they become more involved in the group process, they are inspired to work on relationships *outside of the group*. They begin to take out into the world what they have learned, because they have a place of safety and refuge to return to as they make changes in their lives.

A higher level of risk taking and a greater depth of disclosure happen now. The atmosphere in the group becomes warmer and more relaxed. People freely laugh and cry together. There is a growing commitment to each other that leads them to be more accepting *and* more confrontative. In highly functional groups the roles become fluid. Leaders become followers and followers become leaders.

Group is an exciting arena. At its best the group is a place where people learn who they are and who they want to become. They learn that different people will respond to them in different ways. Perhaps most importantly group members learn to *accept*, because they first were accepted. They now take a leading role in a life lived more joyfully.

Stages in the Life of a Group

Stage 1: Checking it Out

Characteristics:

The group members simultaneously are attracted to the group and anxious about it. They tend either to wait and see or to test out the group. Although there's a desire for intimacy, there's also resistance to anything personal. Most discussion is of the past or the future with the here and now avoided.

Group Leader Tasks:

Accept and welcome everyone. Invite trust and confidence by displaying openness. Answer questions fully and share high expectations for the group. Provide structured activities for members to get to know each other.

Stage II: Where Do I Fit?

Characteristics:

Group members sometimes attempt to define a position for themselves within the group. This can lead to the establishment of a hierarchy. Scapegoating of members may occur as others try to feel more secure.

Group Leader Tasks:

Establish the worth of each person through your interactions. Provide a safe environment where people are protected from attack or rejection. Help group members focus on their similarities rather than their differences. Provide opportunities to appreciate and understand each other.

Stage III: Getting Involved

Characteristics:

Group members begin to reveal themselves as trust and acceptance develop. Risk taking becomes more frequent, and self-disclosure becomes more comfortable. Members often begin to identify as family, sometimes establishing their own traditions.

Group Leader Tasks:

Provide support and encouragement as members risk becoming known to the group. Help group members understand and accept their feelings as they begin to explore issues. Allow the group to take more responsibility for its direction while providing leadership if it gets sidetracked.

Stage IV: Building Bridges

Characteristics:

Sharing becomes deeper and more meaningful. Members appreciate each other as unique. Feelings of closeness are openly expressed even as feedback and confrontation increase. The group may achieve cohesion with members displaying support, acceptance, and affection for each other. The beginnings of change occur within the group members.

Group Leader Tasks:

Assist group members in transferring what they have learned during the group into their relationships while providing a safety net of support. Continue to develop and expand the emotional bridges between group members.

Stage V: Letting Go

Characteristics:

As the group comes to a close, members react in different ways. Most group members value the experience to the end while some will deny that it was ever important. Others resist the ending by insisting they will always be this close. Some groups regress to earlier stages, moving apart prematurely. Other groups help each other in preparing to move on.

Group Leader Tasks:

Help group members identify ways they can extend their experience. Provide support systems by sharing phone numbers or by identifying other groups or community resources. Plan a special last group session. Help the group members evaluate their experience and determine their goals and direction.

Tips for Group Leaders

1. **Model the behaviors you want to see in your group.** Set the tone and teach by example. Demonstrate warmth, acceptance, caring, and interest in each of your group members.

2. **Keep the group sitting close together and in a circle.** Having the group sit in a circle increases their interaction with each other. Each person is in the front row, so to speak, and in a position of equal importance.

3. **Give recognition.** Learn each person's name and use it. If you forget a name, ask. Notice whether group members know each other's names.

4. **Have a plan for the group session.** Always have an activity or discussion planned but without being rigid. Be flexible when the needs of group members surface. The value of group activities is the opportunity they provide for interaction. However, the *purpose* of the group is to give its members a place to talk about what they're experiencing.

5. **Be patient.** Understand that the group process may be a new experience. Allow for silence within your group. Remember that group members will need a few moments to decide how they want to respond or as they search for the words to express themselves.

6. **Encourage everyone to participate.** Even when group members pass during discussions, continue to invite them to share. Watch body language for clues that a normally quiet member is ready to participate. Avoid letting anyone dominate the group. Say, *"Thank you for sharing. Let's hear what the other group members have to add."*

7. **Encourage group members to interact with each other.** Avoid being the answer source. Rather than responding to every question say, *"What do the rest of you think?"* Observe the lines of communication. Who do they look at when they talk? Who talks, how often, and for how long? Who responds?

8. **Keep the focus on the person speaking.** Avoid letting people take the focus away from the one speaking. They often will respond, *"I've had exactly the same thing happen, and I...."* Have them wait until the person has expressed feelings and explored connections. *Then* it's of great value for others to share similar experiences.

9. **Help group members see their similarities.** Notice when people seem to be identifying with the statements of another group member. Encourage them to talk about it when the first one is finished.

10. **Avoid asking why?** Why questions lead to analyzing behavior rather than exploring feelings. Instead ask, *"How were you feeling when you did that?"* or *"What did you hope would happen?"*

11. **Focus on feelings.** Go from experience to feelings by asking questions such as, *"When that happened how did you feel?"* Pay as much attention to tone of voice and body language as to the actual words used.

12. **Understand the value and purpose of group work.** Groups often are uplifting, but they can be heart-rending as well. No value comes from a group that won't deal with topics because they're "too depressing." This only forces people to conceal what they came to release. Truly uplifting experiences come from releasing old, painful feelings.

13. **WRAP during each group session.**

    Warm-up or energizer

    Review of the last group session

    Activity or group discussion

    Process the group session

Giving (and Receiving) Feedback

Some of the most important information people can give, or receive, consists of *feedback* about behavior. Feedback is a special kind of communication that helps people be more aware of what they do and how it affects others. Feedback is like having someone hold a mirror so we can see ourselves more clearly.

Here are guidelines for giving feedback:

Focus feedback on the behavior rather than the person.

Effective feedback refers to what people do rather than to what you think. It's more effective to say, *"That's the third time you've interrupted me today"* rather than *"You're a loud-mouth and don't care about anyone else."*

Focus feedback on observation rather than interpretation.

Observations refer to the things people can see or hear while interpretations refer to their own conclusions. So it's more helpful to say, *"You're very quiet today"* rather than *"You're very depressed today."*

Focus feedback on behavior during a specific, recent situation.

Feedback is most meaningful when it is specific and includes examples. It needs to come as soon as possible after the event to free it from the distortion of time. This prevents disagreements on what did or did not happen. So it's more effective to say, *"When we were discussing group guidelines today, you disagreed with every comment I made"* rather than *"You're too bossy in group."*

Focus feedback on sharing information rather than on giving advice.

When information is shared people decide for themselves how it can be used. Advice states that this is what a person should do. So it's more helpful to say, *"At first I didn't talk much either. I wasn't sure how people would react. But I've learned that this group is really understanding"* rather than *"You should talk more during group."*

Focus feedback on its value to the recipient.

The purpose of feedback is to provide information that's helpful to people or may improve your relationship with them. It's a good idea to verify that your feedback was received the way it was intended. One way is to have people rephrase what you said to see if what they heard is what you meant. It's often good to check with others on the accuracy of the feedback. Is it one person's impression or an impression shared by others?

Feedback sometimes tells us more about the person giving it than it tells us about ourselves. Just because a person says it doesn't make it so. Our strength in receiving feedback is in being open to the truth of what is said, while disregarding the false. Our strength also is in being open to another person's perception as this increases our understanding *of them.*

Giving (and receiving) feedback requires genuine concern, courage, and commitment. When we learn to give and receive it graciously, our relationships deepen and are strengthened by it.

Ground Rules for Group

1. Everything that happens or is said in this group is confidential.

2. Everyone has the right to "pass" on any question or activity.

3. It's your right to speak freely and openly. It's also important to respect each person's right to talk without interruption and to have an equal share of the time.

4. Be aware of feelings in the group. Recognize your feelings and help others do the same.

5. Avoid making judgments. It's hard enough being ourselves without having others put us down.

6. Demonstrate that other group members are important by listening when they talk and by working to understand what they say.

7. Decisions require group consensus, meaning that everyone in the group must be willing to support them.

8. We're here to support each other. Killer statements are not tolerated, whether directed at yourself or others.

9. Commit to be at group each time and on time. When you're not here, it leaves a gap no one else can fill.

10. Everyone who is here belongs and is welcome.

Peer Support Group
Confidentiality Contract

My signature on this contract is my word that I will maintain as confidential everything that is said or that happens with any member of this group.

If I break or am aware of a break in confidentiality, I agree to abide by the following rules and consequences that have been established by my group:

Rules and Consequences:

_____

Group member signature

_____

Date

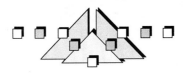

Chapter 18
Group Activities

Activity 1

What is This Group About Anyway?

Introductions:

Group members introduce themselves by giving an adjective that starts with the same letter or sound as their name, for example "Christmas Carol." Ask them to choose an adjective that tells something about them. The first person gives his or her adjective/name, then the second person gives an adjective/name and repeats the first one, continuing around the circle until the last person gives an adjective/name and repeats the adjective/name of each group member.

Or, ask people to say their names and describe themselves with two truths and a lie. For example, *"I like to snow ski, I like to play chess, and I like to cook."* The group tries to guess which are the two truths and which is the lie.

Or, ask people to form pairs getting with the person they know least. They each have five minutes to learn as much as possible about their partner. When time is called, they introduce their partners to the group.

Schedule:

Discuss meeting times and any other details, such as taking roll. If group members will miss class to come to group, suggest strategies for handling this responsibly. Decide if the group wants reminders and how they will be delivered.

Group Discussion:

Group members will want to know what to expect from the group. Make a statement like this, putting it into your own words:

"This group is a place to get to know others and ourselves better. We've got lots of activities to get us started, but they're not what this group is about. Group is about having a place to talk about our lives—what's happening, how we feel, what we need.

"We have to trust each other to do that. So we have some ground rules we'd like to discuss and a confidentiality contract we'll ask you to sign.

"If you've never been in a group before, you're in for a great experience. There's nothing like being with people who support you and who understand how you feel because they've been there, too."

Ground Rules:

Give a copy of "Ground Rules For Group" to each member. Ask if there are any other guidelines they'd like to add. If there is consensus, add it to the list.

Go around the circle and ask people to talk about: (1) the rule that is most important to them, and (2) the rule they'll have the most trouble following.

Confidentiality:

Ask if anyone has ever trusted someone who broke that trust. Ask them to talk about how they felt.

Help the group develop their rules and consequences for dealing with a break in confidentiality. Be sure one of the rules describes what to do if they know another member has broken confidentiality. Make sure there is consensus on the rules and consequences.

Give a copy of the "Peer Support Group Confidentiality Contract" to the group members. Have them write down the rules and consequences the group has adopted before they sign the contract. Collect the contracts to keep as long as the group continues to meet.

Process:

- Are there any questions?
- How do you feel?
- Will you be back?

Activity 2

Past Histories

People in a group often have histories with each other, meaning they've formed an opinion or impression. In a group from the same school, many of the group members will have histories. If their histories are positive or neutral, it won't interfere with developing trust. However, if their histories are negative, this will have a profound influence on how the group relates. Negative feelings will lie just below the surface but never be discussed. Any deep bonding within the group is impossible with this undercurrent.

After giving this explanation, go around the circle asking each person to talk about the histories they share with other members of the group:

If the history is *positive or neutral*, ask the group members to share a short description of the relationship or situation.

If the history is *negative*, ask the group members to talk about:

     1. _____ what *they* will need to do, and

     2. ____ what they will need from the other person.

Process:

- How did you feel discussing histories, both positive and negative?
- How hard is it for you to deal with negative feelings?
- What would have happened if we had never discussed this?

Activity 3

Go-Arounds

Go-arounds are a wonderful way to warm-up a group and insure that each person participates. The group leader or one of the group members can be in charge of choosing (or inventing) the go-around for the group.

1. Tell how you're feeling on a scale from one to ten, with ten being terrific.

2. Share a personal "high" or "low" since the last group session.

3. Tell about a significant goal that directs your life.

4. Share something important you've discovered about yourself recently.

5. When was the last time you tried a new behavior? What happened?

6. Observe three minutes of silence. Talk about what was going on inside you and what you observed in the group.

7. Describe yourself as an animal, a flower, and a song. Explain.

8. If you inherited a million dollars, what would you do with it? How much could you do *without* a million dollars?

9. Talk about the last time someone didn't listen to you.

10. Who is the most important person in your life? What is your relationship?

11. What is the characteristic in people that you most admire?

12. Complete this sentence: *"I used to be... but now I'm...."*

13. If you knew you were going to die in 24 hours, how would you spend your time?

14. What is the worst thing one person can do to another?

15. If you could go back and change one thing you've done, what would it be?

16. Will you raise your children the same way you were raised?

17. If you could wake up tomorrow with a new ability or talent, what would it be?

18. Five years from now, how might you feel about the things you do now? What might you wish you had changed?

19. When was the last time you cried? Tell us what happened.

20. Name a role model. What do you admire about this person?

21. What feelings do you have the most trouble expressing?

22. Complete this statement: *"A turning point in my life was...."*

23. How would you describe yourself to someone who doesn't know you?

24. What do you like most about yourself? What do you dislike?

25. What is a risk for personal growth you will take this week?

Process:

- Who did you learn the most about today?
- What would you like to ask someone?
- What else would you like to share?

Activity 4

Stringing Along

The group leader holds a ball of string or yarn. When the group discussion begins, the group leader holds the end of the string and tosses the ball of string to the first person that speaks. This person holds onto his section of string and tosses the ball of string to the next person that speaks, and so on.

The group examines the network formed by the string when the discussion ends.

Process:

- Who spoke most frequently? Who spoke least?
- What patterns of response do you see?
- What can we all do to help each member participate fully?

Activity 5

Tell Us Your Life Story—
You Have One Minute

The group selects one of its members to present a one-minute autobiography. This person may do anything to get the group members to listen, while the group may do anything *not* to listen.

After the first person has finished, choose 1 or 2 other group members to present autobiographies.

Allow the autobiographers to discuss their frustration at talking about something important and having no one listen. What were the different ways people used not to listen? Although this was intentional, how do we do this unintentionally?

Go around the circle with this question: *"Why are you in this group?"* What personal characteristics do you want to change, what relationships do you want to improve, or what do you hope to gain?

Process:

- What similarities exist among group members?
- Whose situation seems most like yours? Did you know this?
- Who would you like to talk with more?

Activity 6

The Outsider

Form small groups of 3 or 4 members. Then each small group decides who will be the outsider.

The small groups form a tight circle, linking arms and facing the middle of the circle. They have formed a clique. As the outsider tries to break into the clique, they respond as a clique would respond. Give them a few moments to discuss this.

The outsiders *really* want in the clique and may do any-thing—short of violence—to break in or be accepted.

Give the signal for the outsiders to begin. Allow about a minute. Then a different person from the small group is chosen to be the outsider. Continue this until every person has experienced being the outsider.

Process:

- How did you feel, both as the insider and outsider?
- What methods worked?
- Do people change in trying to become part of a clique?
- How do we unintentionally make others feel like outsiders?
- What are the different groups within this group?

Activity 7

Labels are for Cans, Not People

People often relate to each other based on labels. To experience this, group members have a label placed on them where they can't see it. Their label instructs others how to respond to them. The group members walk around the room, talking to each person. They are to talk about a time when they made someone angry but didn't mean to.

Two things will happen: When Person A speaks to Person B, Person B responds to Person A's label. When Person B speaks to Person A, Person A responds to Person B's label.

Process:

- How did you change as people responded to you?
- What did you observe? What does this say?
- What are the actual labels some people wear?

Labels

Walk away when I talk.
Tell me I'm stupid.
Smile and welcome me.
Ask my opinion.
Don't trust me.
Help me.
Ask about my hair and clothes.
Misunderstand me.
Just stare at me.
Admire me.
Look at my left shoulder when I talk.
Laugh at me.
Criticize what I say.
Yell when I use the word "I."
Pity me.
Ignore me.
Care about me.
Interrupt me.
Step back when I speak.
Loudly repeat what I tell you.

Activity 8

Between the Sexes

Inner Circle:

The females form a circle, facing the middle of the circle.

Outer Circle:

The males form a circle around the females, also facing the middle of the circle.

The inner circle is given a question to discuss for 3 to 5 minutes. The outer circle listens quietly. Then the outer circle discusses *the same question* for 3 to 5 minutes while the inner circle listens quietly.

Note: Group members are to save comments and questions for the opposite circle until the end.

When the next question is chosen, the outer circle begins first. Continue to alternate with each new question.

Questions:

- What are some things males don't understand about females?
- What are some things females don't understand about males?
- What is the best thing you've learned from your male friends?
- What is the best thing you've learned from your female friends?
- What do males look for in a date? In an ideal partner?
- What do females look for in a date? In an ideal partner?
- What is the most creative date you can imagine?
- Who should ask for a date? Who pays?
- How do you like to be approached?
- What do you do when you don't want to date someone?
- How do you handle someone who pressures you?
- What is most difficult in relating to males? To females?

Process:

- What did you learn about the opposite sex?
- What did you learn about yourself?
- What needs to be talked about more?

Activity 9

1 See, I Know, I Believe

Group members form pairs, choosing the person they know least.

The group members make a series of *"I see..."* statements to their partner. These statements are limited to things they can see about their partner. For example:

- *"I see you have blue eyes."*
- *"I see you're smiling."*
- *"I see you're wearing a ring."*

Next the group members make a series of *"I know..."* statements. These statements are limited to things they know are true of their partner. For example:

- *"I know you live with your mother."*
- *"I know you've got Mr. Brown for math."*
- *"I know we've never talked before."*

Last the group members make a series of *"I believe..."* statements. These statements are based on what they believe is true of their partner. For example:

- *"I believe you're smart."*
- *"I believe you're a good friend."*
- *"I believe you're shy."*

Process:

- How did this feel?
- What did you learn?
- How is what others *see, know,* and *believe* different from your perception?

Activity 10

Inner Circle, Outer Circle

The group leader gives these instructions:

"Please divide into two equal groups. One group will form a small inner circle *facing out*. The other group will form an outer circle *facing in*. When you're in position, each person will be facing a partner.

"We're going to use the skills of communicating *and* listening in this activity. When I give the signal, each person in the inner circle will complete the statement, *'I am...'* continuing to give additional responses for 1 minute. For example, I might say, *'I am a senior, I am a friend, I am a peer helper, I am a person who cares about people...'* and so on until time is called.

"Partners in the outer circle are to listen. If your partner gets stuck, you can say things such as, *'And what else are you?'* Please begin.

"Stop please. Partners in the Outer Circle, repeat everything your partner said. You have 30 seconds.

"Now you'll switch roles with the partner in the outer circle completing the statement, *'I am...'* continuing to give additional responses for 1 minute. Please begin.

"Stop please. Partners in the Inner Circle, repeat everything your partner said.

"Now I'd like the people in the outer circle to move two positions to your right.... This time we'll have the people in the outer circle begin by completing the statement, *'I feel...'* continuing to give additional responses for one minute. For example, I might say, *'I feel accepted in this group, I feel happy when I make someone laugh, I feel saddened by racism...'* and so on until time is called. Please begin.

"Stop please. Partners in the Inner Circle, repeat everything your partner said.

"Now switch roles with the partner in the inner circle completing the statement, *'I feel...'* continuing to give additional responses for 1 minute. Please begin.

"Stop please. Partners in the Outer Circle, repeat everything your partner said.

"Again I'd like the people in the outer circle to move two positions to your right.... The people in the inner circle will begin this round by completing the statement, *'I need...'* continuing to give additional responses for 1 minute. For example, I might say, *'I need to get more sleep, I need be more open with my parents, I need to do my homework...'* and so on until time is called. Please begin.

"Stop please. Partners in the Outer Circle, repeat everything your partner said.

"Now switch roles with the partner in the outer circle completing the statement, *'I need...'* continuing to give additional responses for 1 minute. Please begin.

"Stop please. Partners in the Inner Circle, repeat everything your partner said."

Process:

- Which was harder for you, speaking or listening?
- Who was an especially good listener?
- Who was especially open?

Activity 11

First Impressions

The group members write down five first impressions they believe others have of them.

Then they write down a first impression they had of each person in the group.

When a member volunteers, the other group members share their first impression. Then volunteers read the list of five first impressions they believe others have of them.

Process:

- How similar are the first impressions of others and what you believed?
- If different, what would explain this?
- Do you want to change any impressions others have? What will you begin doing?

Activity 12

Extremes

This activity allows group members to declare their positions on several issues. They respond to each question by physically positioning themselves on an imaginary line going from one corner of the room to the opposite corner.

When a question is read, the leader indicates the location of each extreme.

For example, *"How often do you talk to people you don't know?"*

The leader says, "If your answer is *always*, stand here (indicates one corner). If your answer is *never*, stand here (indicates the opposite corner). If your answer is in between, position yourself where you feel you belong."

Process:

When the group members are in position, they tell the people on both sides of them:

1. Their reasons for choosing that position, and

2. How they feel about where they are.

The people at opposite ends of the imaginary line talk to each other across the room, discussing their responses.

"How far will you go to be accepted by others?"
Extremes: I will do anything—I will do nothing
"How do you feel about marriage?"
Extremes: I want to marry as soon as possible—I will never get married
"What is most important to you in a romantic relationship?"
Extremes: Being best friends—Physical attraction
"What is the most important use of life?"
Extremes: Making money—Helping others
"How close are you to your family?"
Extremes: We are best friends—We are like strangers
"How do you feel about yourself?"
Extremes: I like myself—I don't like myself
"How do you feel about people?"
Extremes: I trust everyone—I trust no one

Activity 13

My Mother, My Father, My Self

The group members describe themselves as:

1. Their mother sees them.
2. Their father sees them.
3. They see themselves.
4. They would like to become.

Process:

- What will it take to be the person you want to become?
- What can you begin doing with your mother? Your father?
- What do you realize for the first time?

Activity 14

Self-Portrait

Group members "draw a picture" by choosing five words from the list to describe them.

Ask them to tell the group:

1. Which descriptive words they chose.
2. What they *do* that makes the words accurate.
3. What they get out of being that way.

Then group members choose three words they *wish* described them.

Have them tell the group:

1. What people *do* who are like that.
2. How it would change their life.

Members also may ask the group to pick five words they feel describe them. Have the group members give specific examples to show the accuracy of the words they choose.

Process:

- What do you see differently?
- What did you learn about how you're perceived?
- What will you begin doing?

Some Descriptive Words

Forgiving	Boring	Moody
Selfish	Extroverted	Depressed
Stimulating	Indifferent	Trusting
Open	Giving	Funny
Angry	Follower	Leader
Assertive	Affectionate	Sympathetic
Shy	Aloof	Nervous
Thoughtful	Opinionated	Creative
Understanding	Judgmental	Enthusiastic
Sensitive	Aggressive	Sentimental
Distracted	Confident	Competitive
Accepting	Attentive	Quiet
Serious	Forgetful	Honest
Loyal	Talkative	Thoughtless
Mellow	Generous	Dependable

Activity 15

A Focus on Feelings

List the following feelings on a chalkboard or pad of paper:

Anger

Fear

Happiness

Jealousy

Sadness

Guilt

Love

Shame

Hatred

Loneliness

Hope

Have the group members form pairs. They each are to identify the feeling they experience most frequently. Have them tell their partner about the most recent situation in which they felt this way. Give them several minutes to discuss this.

Then the group leader explains that our feelings are caused by the way we think about an event, giving several examples to illustrate this.

Ask group members to identify the *thoughts* they had with the feeling they described to their partner. Give them several minutes to discuss this.

Process:

- What did you discover?
- What other feelings could you choose?
- In what other situations could you choose to feel differently?

Activity 16

Self-Disclosure

The group leader introduces the activity with a statement like this:

"Most of us are afraid of not being accepted, so we *hide* who we are and how we feel. Ironically it works in just the opposite way. When we're closed, people misunderstand and tend to reject us. But when we're open about who we are and how we feel, people accept us because they can understand us.

"It's a tremendous relief to share what we've kept inside. Keeping it secret allows it to control us.

"Most of us have a typical behavior we use in situations where we're afraid, embarrassed, ashamed, or feel inadequate. Those behaviors are:

Silence:

If I don't say anything, no one will find out who I am.

Joking:

If I keep them laughing, no one will find out who I am.

Acting superior:

If I act like this is stupid, no one will find out who I am.

Acting confused:

If I act like I don't understand, no one will find out who I am."

Ask your group members to identify the behavior they tend to use. Invite them to share what it is they're afraid others will find out about them.

Process:

- Who would you like to encourage?
- Who helped you the most with their sharing?
- What will you do differently?

Activity 17

Proud Moments

The group leader makes a statement like this:

"It's hard to talk about our accomplishments. Most people have been taught not to brag, but bragging and quietly feeling good are different.

"Learning to prize the things we do well strengthens us and encourages us. If we focus only on what we *lack*, our image of ourselves becomes as distorted as the one we see in a carnival mirror."

Go around the circle and ask group members to share a proud moment.

Process:

- Was this hard for you?
- What do you appreciate about other group members?
- The next time you have a proud moment, will you share it with us?

Activity 18

Secrets

The group leader gives these instructions:

"This activity will demonstrate that others can understand our experiences and feelings. We'll ask each of you to write a secret about yourself on a piece of paper. The secret can be something you've thought or done but should be something you've never told anyone. We'll place the pieces of paper in a container and mix them up. Then we'll each draw one of the secrets out of the container.

"We'll read the secret as if it were our own and talk about how it 'feels.' Please remember that people can role-play only from *their* point of view. It's impossible to know another person's actual experiences and responses. We can only share what *we* would feel.

"We'd also like other group members who have had a similar experience to talk about it when the person is finished."

Note: It is *essential* that group members be at a stage of development where they can respond in caring and empathic ways for this activity.

Process:

- How did you feel role-playing another person's secret?
- How did you feel about the way the group responded?
- What does this make you realize?

Activity 19

Asking for Feedback

Group members choose a question from the list below, or they may ask their own question. They may choose the person they want to answer their question or open it to the entire group.

The group leader first discusses the guidelines for giving and receiving feedback.

Questions:

What do you think is my best quality?
What is something that you don't understand about me?
How would you describe me?.
What kind of person do you think I get along with best?
What is a strength and a weakness of mine?
In what ways am I good with people?
What do you like best about me? Least?
What do you see me doing in ten years?
How well do I deal with anger?
What seems to be difficult for me? What comes easily?
How accepting am I?
What do I seem to enjoy most?
What do you think hurts me the most?
How have I changed since this group began?
What is something you have always wanted to tell me?
What do you wish I would do?
What can I do to help you trust me more?
How do I make you feel?
How have I influenced you during this group?
What will you always remember about me?

Process:

- Which is harder, giving or receiving feedback?
- How do you feel about the feedback you received?
- Is there something else you would like to ask?

Activity 20

Get-My-Way Behaviors

Group members form pairs. One takes the role of the "have." The other takes the role of the "have not." Give them a moment to decide who will take each role.

Then the group leader gives these instructions:

"The *haves* have something the *have nots* want. But the haves refuse to give it to the have nots. It doesn't matter what 'it' is. What matters is that the haves won't give it to the have nots.

"Have nots, you *really* want it, and you're going to try to convince your partner to give it to you. You may use any method of persuasion except one. You may not touch your partner.

"Haves, you are to respond in whatever way seems appropriate or natural to you.

"Have nots, you have one minute to get it from your partner."

When time is called, the partners switch roles with the have becoming the new have not.

The group leader continues:

"Although this is a simulation, you can learn about your personal style in dealing with conflict by observing how you responded here. Most people respond to this simulation in much the same way they respond to *life situations*. If we analyzed the methods people used, most of them would fall into one of three categories: passive, aggressive, or assertive."

The group leader uses "Styles of Interaction: Passive, Aggressive, and Assertive" to describe these behaviors to the group.

Ask the group members to discuss which style of interaction is their predominant one.

Process:

- Did you already know your style?
- Does your style of interaction work for you?
- Is there a different style you would like to develop?

Activity 21

Flat Earth Society

The group leader says, "Please stand and repeat after me:

> I, (state your name), being of sound mind and body, (or almost sound mind and body), do hereby declare myself, to be a member, in good standing, of the Flat Earth Society, of the United States of America."

The group leader continues:

"Until late in the fifteenth century people believed the Earth was flat. When sailors went out on the ocean, they kept land in sight at all times because they were afraid of sailing off the edge of the Earth. It was only after Columbus, Magellan, and others completed their voyages that people understood the Earth was not flat, but round.

"However, not everyone accepted this new information. There were people who clung to the belief that the Earth was flat *in spite of overwhelming evidence to the contrary.* Today there are still people who believe the Earth is flat, and they're referred to as the Flat Earth Society.

"However, when we continue behaviors we know to be unhealthy, *we're doing the same thing.* We're going to call these 'flat Earth behaviors.'

"In spite of overwhelming evidence that smoking will kill you through lung cancer, heart disease, and emphysema, people continue to smoke. In spite of overwhelming evidence that cocaine has deadly consequences, thousands use cocaine every day in this country.

"What are other examples of flat Earth behaviors, perhaps some that you do?"

(These could include heavy drinking, driving under the influence, unprotected sex, overexposure to the sun, eating junk food, not being able to say no, and so on.)

Ask the group members to name as many flat Earth behaviors as they can. Then ask them to *pick the one* that influences them the most, the one that would change their life if they changed their behavior.

Process:

- Will you change your flat Earth behavior? What action will you take?
- What level of intention will you bring to it?
- Who will be your accountability partner?

Action Plan

Flat Earth Behavior _____

What healthy behavior will replace it?

Goal _____

How will you get there?

Step by Step

Today _____

This week _____

This month _____

Six months _____

A year _____

What might get in the way?

Obstacles _____

_____

_____

How will you know when you've reached your goal?

New Behaviors _____

_____

_____

Target Date _____

I, _____, am committed
to this plan of action.   Date _____

_____   _____
Accountability Partner   Date

Activity 22

Strength Bombardment

These activities are excellent for bringing closure to a group before a major holiday or at the end of the year. They also can be used to give group members positive strokes at any time of the year.

1. The group leader gives the members a piece of paper for each person in the group. The group members write a message to each person in the group. The messages are to be as specific as possible, focusing on an ability or characteristic of the person that the writer enjoys or admires.

2. The group leader tapes a paper plate or blank sheet of paper on each group member's back. The group members move about the room, writing a special message to each person.

3. The group leader asks a group member to act as record keeper. The group member on the record keeper's right becomes the target of a positive bombardment. Each of the group members says a word or phrase that describes something special about the person. The record keeper makes a list of all the words and phrases given. When everyone has responded, the list is passed around and the group members sign next to their word or phrase.

4. Each person becomes the target of a strength bombardment for 10 to 15 minutes. The group members share positive feedback in any form they choose. They may share stories about the person, talk about something the person has done to influence their life, or describe ways they admire the person. At the end of the strength bombardment, the target has one minute to respond.

Section V
Classroom Presentations

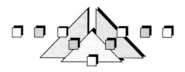

Chapter 19
Fourth Grade Substance Abuse Prevention Program

Session I

I. Introductions

Do introductions and explain what it means to be a peer helper.

Tell the students that you'll be with them four sessions talking about very important ideas.

In *this* session you'll be talking about how important it is to feel good about yourself.

In the *second* session you'll be talking about feelings and how important it is to talk about them.

In the *third* session you'll be talking about being a better listener and learning to communicate better.

In the *fourth* session you'll be talking about substance abuse. People sometimes use alcohol or other drugs as a way to feel good when they don't talk about their feelings and when it's hard for them to communicate.

II. Warm Fuzzies

Read the story, *Warm Fuzzies (and Cold Pricklies)*.

Ask the students to give examples of warm fuzzies and cold pricklies.

III. Process

Which are more common, warm fuzzies or cold pricklies? Why is this?

Which is harder, giving or receiving a warm fuzzy?

What happens when people get a warm fuzzy? What about a cold prickly?

What happens to people who get cold pricklies all the time

Does anyone have a story about a time you gave a warm fuzzy (or cold prickly) to someone?

IV. Challenge

Keep track of how many warm fuzzies and cold pricklies you give this week. Notice how *you feel* when you give warm fuzzies and cold pricklies.

V. Question Box

Leave a question box in the room for any questions the students are not comfortable asking in class. Tell them you'll go through the questions each week and answer as many as possible.

Thank the teacher and students for having you as a guest. Make sure they know when you'll return.

Warm Fuzzies (and Cold Pricklies)

Long ago only little people lived on the Earth. They lived in the village of Swabeedoo, and so they called themselves Swabeedoo-dahs. They were very happy little people, and they went around with big smiles and cheerful greetings.

What the Swabeedoo-dahs enjoyed most was giving warm fuzzies to each other. Each of them carried a shoulder bag, and these bags were always filled with warm fuzzies. Whenever two Swabeedoo-dahs would meet, they would give each other a warm fuzzy. It was a way of saying, "Hello. I like you." It felt *really good* to get so many warm fuzzies. It made each of the Swabeedoo-dahs feel noticed and appreciated, and then they wanted to give more warm fuzzies in return. This made their lives together very happy indeed.

Outside the village in a cold, dark cave lived a great green troll. He didn't really like to live all by himself, and he was lonely sometimes. But he couldn't seem to get along with anyone, and he definitely didn't like exchanging warm fuzzies.

"It's just not cool," he said.

One evening the troll walked into town and was greeted by a kindly little Swabeedoo-dah. "Hasn't this been a fine Swabeedoo-dah day?" said the little person with a smile. "Here have a warm fuzzy. This one is special. I saved it just for you."

The troll looked around to make sure no one else was listening. Then he whispered in the little Swabeedoo-dah's ear, "Haven't you heard that if you give away too many warm fuzzies, one of these days you're gonna run out?"

He saw the look of surprise and fear on the little Swabeedoo-dah's face. Then he added, "Right now, I'd say you've got about seventy-three warm fuzzies in your fuzzybag there. Better go easy on givin' em away!" With that the troll padded away on his big green feet, leaving a very worried and confused Swabeedoo-dah standing there.

Now the troll knew there was an unending supply of warm fuzzies. He knew that as soon as you give a warm fuzzy another one comes to take its place, and you can never, ever run out of warm fuzzies in your whole life. But he counted on the trusting nature of the little Swabeedoo-dahs. So he told his fib and went back to his cave and waited.

Well, he didn't have long to wait. The first person to come along and greet the little Swabeedoo-dah was an old friend of his. His friend was surprised to find that when he gave a warm fuzzy, he received only a strange look in return and was told to beware of running out of warm fuzzies. That same afternoon the friend told seven other Swabeedoo-dahs who told nineteen other Swabeedoo-dahs, "Sorry, no warm fuzzy this time. I'm a little low."

By the next day word had spread over the entire village. Everyone had suddenly begun to save their warm fuzzies. They still gave some away, but only occasionally.

"Very carefully," they said.

The little Swabeedoo-dahs began to be suspicious of each other and to hide their bags of warm fuzzies under their pillows at night. People even began to trade warm fuzzies for things, instead of giving them away. There even were reports of robberies of warm fuzzies. Some nights it wasn't safe to be out and about.

At first the troll was pleased. Now when he went into town, he was no longer greeted with smiles or offered warm fuzzies. Instead the little people looked at him the way they looked at each other, *suspiciously.* He rather liked that. To him that was just facing reality.

"It's the way the world is," he said.

But things kept getting worse. More and more Swabeedoo-dahs came down with a disease known as "hardening of the heart," and a few of the little people died. Now all the happiness was gone from the village of Swabeedoo.

When the troll heard what was happening, he said to himself, "Gosh! I just wanted them to see how the world is. I didn't mean for 'em to die!" He kept wondering what he should do. Then he thought of a plan.

Deep in his cave the troll had discovered a secret mine of cold pricklies. He had spent many years digging the cold pricklies out of the mountain because he liked their cold and prickly feel. He decided to share them with the Swabeedoo-dahs. He filled hundreds of bags with cold pricklies and took them into the village.

When the people saw the bags of cold pricklies, they were relieved and took them gratefully. At least now they had something to give each other. The only trouble was it just wasn't as much fun to give a cold prickly. *Getting* a cold prickly gave you a funny feeling, too. It was nice to get something from people, but it was hard to know for sure what they meant. After all, cold pricklies *are* cold and prickly.

Some of the Swabeedoo-dahs went back to giving warm fuzzies. Each time a warm fuzzy was exchanged, it made both of the little people very happy. Perhaps that was partly because it was so unusual to get a warm fuzzy, with so many cold pricklies being exchanged.

But giving warm fuzzies never really came back into style in Swabeedoo. A few of the little people found they could keep giving away warm fuzzies without ever running out. But the *art* of giving warm fuzzies had been lost in Swabeedoo.

Now suspicion was in the minds of the little people. You could hear it in their voices. *"Warm fuzzy, huh. Wonder what he wants from me?"*

> *Author Unknown*
> *Condensed and Revised*

Based on *The Original Warm Fuzzy Tale,* by Claude Steiner

Session II

I. Challenge Report

Ask the students what they discovered from the challenge.

Review your discussion of warm fuzzies and cold pricklies. Explain that you're going to talk more about feelings during this session.

II. "Feelings" Demonstration

Ask for five volunteers. Give each volunteer a piece of paper with one of the following directions: Show A Tired Walk, Show An Angry Walk, Show A Happy Walk, Show A Frightened Walk, and Show A Sad Walk. After each demonstration, ask the class to guess what feeling was shown.

Ask: *"But how can you know the feelings since no words were used?"*

Explain that we communicate even when we don't use words. However, remind them of the times they guessed the wrong feeling. Explain that if we want people to understand how we feel, we have to tell them.

III. "Show Me" Story

Ask for five new volunteers. Tell the volunteers you're going to read a short story. Each time you pause, you want the volunteer to show how he or she would be feeling if that was happening. The first time you pause, you want the first volunteer to show the feeling, and so on.

"Let me tell you a story about my terrible day at school... (pause).... The first thing that happened was that everyone laughed at me because of my haircut... (pause).... I was so upset, I didn't hear the bell ring... (pause).... When I came running in late, everyone laughed at me again... (pause).... When my teacher said I had to stay in at recess, I was mad... (pause).... All morning everything I did turned out wrong... (pause).... But during recess my teacher talked to me, and then I felt so much better... (pause).... I still don't like my haircut, but I know it'll grow out... (pause).... And you know what? Some of my friends said they like my haircut... (pause).... They said they like *me,* so what difference does it make?... (pause)....

IV. Identify Feelings

Ask the class to list the feelings shown during the demonstration. (The list may include: angry, sad, happy, afraid, confused, depressed, worried, lonely, hurt.) Write the list on the board where it can remain during the next part of the presentation.

V. Recognize Feelings

Explain that we must learn to *recognize* what we're feeling, and our bodies always give us signals.

Ask the students to list the different ways our bodies signal us about our feelings. (The list may include: stomach ache, headache, clenched teeth, clenched fists, stiff neck, red face, tense muscles, crying, heart pounding.) Write this list on the board.

Explain that not everyone reacts the same way to the same feeling. Some people get a headache when they're angry; others get a stomach ache. Ask some of the students to connect the feelings that were listed with the list of body reactions. Emphasize that it's learning to recognize *your* reaction that counts.

VI. Express Feelings

There are no good or bad feelings. It's what we *do* about our feelings that can be good or bad. Ask the students to list positive ways to handle feelings. (The list may include: talk to someone, exercise, write in a journal, go for a walk, play with the dog, know it will pass.)

Draw a circle around "talk to someone" and have the students identify the people to whom they can talk.

VII. Process

Why is it important to let people know how you feel?

Why do people sometimes laugh at feelings?

Is there anyone who has decided to talk to someone *today*?

VIII. Challenge

Keep track of how often you cover up and how often you talk about your feelings this week.

IX. Question Box

Answer as many questions as time permits.

Session III

I. Challenge Report

Ask the students what they discovered from the challenge.

Explain that sometimes it's hard for people to talk about feelings because no one listens. Also sometimes it's hard to know what *to say*. Tell the students that you're going to practice both parts of communication.

II. "Listening" Demonstration

1st peer helper:

"Let me tell you about my weekend. It was so much fun! I..."

2nd peer helper:

"I had a great weekend, too!"

1st peer helper:

"Yeah?... good. We went to San Diego, and the weather was just right. We...."

2nd peer helper:

"When the weather's like that, I like to play tennis."

1st peer helper:

"Oh... well, good. I wanted to tell you about San Diego...."

2nd peer helper:

"I remember the last time I was in San Diego. I was in a tennis tournament."

1st peer helper:

"Uhh... that's nice.... We got to go down to the harbor, and we saw some boats...."

2nd peer helper:

"Boating is my next favorite thing after tennis."

1st peer helper:

"Oh? Well... anyway, after that we rode down this winding road right by the ocean...."

2nd peer helper:

"My grandmother lives on a winding road by the ocean!"

1st peer helper:

"Yeah, well, that's nice.... Listen, I'll talk to you later."

III. Process

This was exaggerated, but has anything like this ever happened to you?

How did you feel?

Have you ever *done* this? What happened?

Do you suppose some people don't talk because no one listens? How long will they keep trying?

IV. Communication Activity

There are two parts to communication. One is being a good listener. The other is being willing *to talk* about how you feel.

Ask the students to do some role-plays to demonstrate. Ask for 3 to 5 volunteers for each situation:

Situation 1: John is a new student sitting alone in the cafeteria. Two of his classmates want to make friends, and they sit down at the table with him. But whenever they ask John a question, he turns away and ignores them. Finally they get up and walk away.

Process:

What is the message the two students got from John?

What might John be feeling besides what it seems?

What else could John do? What can the friends do?

Situation 2: A group of classmates teases Anna because she always gets the best grades in the class. Then Anna teases them back about always getting in trouble because they never do their work.

Process:

How do you think Anna feels?

How do you think the ones teasing Anna feel?

What could they do to help each other?

Situation 3: Whenever teams are picked at recess, James is always the last one chosen. He acts like it doesn't bother him, but of course it does. The team captain who gets James says, *"Why do we get James again?"* James says, *"That's okay. I don't really want to play."*

Process:

How do you think James feels?

Which is more important, being a friend or winning?

Can you imagine how much James hates recess? What could you do?

V. Challenge

Be a good listener for three people this week. Talk to someone this week about something bothering you.

VI. Question Box

Answer as many questions as time permits.

Session IV

I. Challenge Report

Ask the students what they discovered from the challenge.

II. Substance Abuse Discussion

Make a statement like this:

"People sometimes start drinking or doing drugs to feel better. The problem is that this doesn't help. The feelings are still there the next day. And people can become addicted, which means they can't stop. Now they have a big problem on top of all the other ones.

"People sometimes start drinking or doing drugs because they're bored or trying to be cool. People sometimes start because their friends talk them into it. This is peer pressure."

Tell the students you want them to make an agreement with you that *they* won't start and that they'll do what they can to see that their friends don't start either.

Explain that they're going to receive a certificate for participating in this program, and it includes an agreement for them to sign. Ask them to wait until everyone has received a certificate before signing theirs. Then individually call the students to the front of the room to receive their certificate. Read the agreement aloud together. Then ask the students to sign and date their certificate.

III. Question Box

Answer as many questions as time permits.

IV. Process

"Since this is our last session, we'd like to do an activity called I Learned...." (Write the words I Learned on the board.) *"We'd like to hear what you've learned during our four sessions with you."*

Write their responses on the board—and add one of yours.

Thank them for being so great. You had fun! Did they?

USA Peer Helper

Fourth Grade
Substance Abuse Prevention Program

This certifies that

_____

has successfully
completed the USA Peer Helper Substance Abuse
Prevention Program.

"I agree that I will never abuse alcohol
or use other drugs.
I also agree to do what I can
to get help for a friend who does."

_____

Signature   Date

_____   _____

Teacher Signature Date   Peer Helper Signature Date

_____   _____

Principal Signature Date   Peer Helper Signature Date

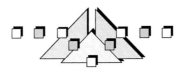

Chapter 20

Transition to the Middle School Program

Part I:
Introduction and Discussion
Differences at the Middle School

Do introductions and explain what you do as a peer helper. Explain that you're there to help prepare them for the middle school next year.

Involve the students in a discussion of the differences they'll experience at the middle school. Include topics such as: using a locker, having a different teacher each hour, and being at a bigger school. Offer positive suggestions and tips for these changes and other concerns raised by the students.

Tell the students that one of the things you worried about when you started middle school was being able to *open your locker*. So you brought several combination locks with you to demonstrate and to practice with them. Share stories of times you had trouble with your lock and how someone helped you.

Discuss the clubs and extracurricular activities listed in the middle school handbook. Share some of your own experiences and activities. Talk about the fun you had and the people you met. Encourage them to get involved.

Part II:
The Story of Kelly

Ask for five volunteers. Let them know they'll be asked to repeat a story. One volunteer remains in the room while the four other volunteers and a peer helper leave. The remaining peer helper reads the "Story Of Kelly" to the first volunteer in front of the class. Then the second volunteer is brought in. The first volunteer tells the story to the second volunteer, who tells it to the third, and so on. The fifth volunteer repeats the story to the class. Then the peer helper rereads the "Story Of Kelly."

Story of Kelly

Kelly is an eighth grader at Canyon Middle School in Tucson, Arizona. She moved to Arizona from California in seventh grade.

Kelly is a friendly person who normally gets along with everyone. But this Monday morning is different. She's getting angry because people keep telling her about her boyfriend, Mark, and her best friend, Angie. Mark's best friend, Ryan, said Mark and Angie were getting along *real good* at the party Friday night. So far eleven people have told Kelly about it. She is hurt and confused but trying not to let it show.

Mr. and Mrs. Roberts, Kelly's parents, had a church activity Friday night, so she had to babysit her brother, Jeffrey, and her little sister, Lisa. Angie knew how much Kelly wanted to go to the party. Kelly doesn't know it, but Angie has liked Mark since sixth grade. The only time Kelly and Angie ever had a fight was right after Kelly moved to the middle school. There was a rumor going around about Kelly, and some people said Angie started it. That was a long time ago, though, and since then Kelly and Angie have been best friends.

Process

Identify the details that were changed.

What does this say about anything repeated several times?

Have you ever had a rumor about you? How did it feel?

Discuss the connection between rumors and fights at the middle school. Ask the students what *they* can do to stop rumors. Talk about the positive ways these situations are handled at the high school.

Part III:
Refusal Skills

Teach the refusal skills to the class, doing 2 or 3 role-plays to demonstrate.

Then divide the class into small groups, with one peer helper to a group. Use the role-play topics as situations. One student is the target of the peer pressure, and the others put on the pressure. After processing the role-play, choose another situation and another student to be the target.

Process:

How did you handle the pressure?

What worked and what didn't work?

What are some actual situations you're dealing with? Let's role-play them.

Refusal Skills

Ways To Say "NO":

1. **Recruit a friend.** Find someone who feels the same way you do.

2. **Be a "broken record."** Use the same phrase over and over. *"No thanks, I don't think I will." "No thanks, I don't think I will."*

3. **Delay**. Stall in making a decision. *"I'll have to see if I can."*

4. **Avoid the situation.** Don't go to the party or leave if things happen that you don't like.

5. **Personal credit.** Use your value as a person. *"Do I have to do that to be your friend?"*

6. **"Chicken" counter attack.** Turn it around. *"I'm not the chicken. I know where I stand."*

7. **Suggest an alternative.** When it's a friend you want to keep, suggest doing something else. *"I don't really want to go to that party. Why don't we get a group together and go ice skating instead?"*

8. **Just say no.** Say it any way you want or give any reason you want.

Role-Play Topics

You don't like school. But you've decided that if you went to school more, maybe you'd do better. Then a buddy says, *"Come on! We can find something better to do than stay in this dump!"* What do you do?

You're at a concert. The three people next to you are smoking pot. Suddenly one of them asks if you want some. You say no. They laugh at you and tease you for being so straight. One of them says you're "chicken." What do you do?

There's this cool girl in your class who hangs around with all the cool kids. You've wanted her to notice you for a long time. One day you run into her at the mall, and she asks if you want to hang out. Later she says, *"This is boring. Let's go out back and have a cigarette."* What do you do?

You and a friend have just gotten out of a movie when one of your neighbors drives up and asks if you want a ride home. You can tell he's been drinking. You're nervous, but you're afraid to make a big deal out of it. What do you do?

You're at your best friend's house, and no one else is home. Your friend, Mike, knows where they keep the booze. He says no one will ever know. He does it all the time. Mike is pouring you a drink, but you really don't want it. What do you do?

You're at the school playing basketball one Saturday morning with your best friend. Suddenly he pulls a can of spray paint out of his backpack and says, *"Let's get even with that jerk, Mr. Smith! We'll write stuff about him on the wall. Come on!"* What do you do?

You and a friend have gone to a school dance. Your friend's older brother picks you up. He asks if you want to go to a party. You say that you have to be home by 10:30. He says, *"Come on, we'll tell them we had car trouble."* What do you do?

Part IV: Closure

Bring the class back together as a group.

Process:

What was the best part of our presentation?

What did you enjoy the most?

What was the most important thing you learned?

Do you have any other questions?

Thank them for being such a great group!

References

Berger, S. (1983). *Divorce without victims: Helping children through divorce with a minimum of pain and trauma.* Boston, MA: Houghton Mifflin.

Canning, J. (1985). *Play times: A structured developmental play program utilizing trained peer facilitators.* Minneapolis, MN: Educational Media Corporation.

Cloud, H., & Townsend, J. (2000). *Boundaries in dating.* Grand Rapids, MI: Zondervan Publishing House.

Cloud, H., & Townsend, J. (1992). *Boundaries.* Grand Rapids, MI: Zondervan Publishing House.

Cranshaw, F. (1997). *Bearing up: Teddy bears as catalysts in caring relationships.* Minneapolis, MN: Educational Media Corporation.

Dunlap, J., & Stewart, J. (1983). *Keeping the fire alive.* Tulsa, OK: PennWell Publishing.

Einstein, E., & Albert, L. (1986). *Strengthening your stepfamily.* Circle Pines, MN: American Guidance Service.

Hafen, B.Q., & Frandsen, K.J. (1986). *Youth suicide: Depression and loneliness.* Evergreen, CO: Cordillera Press.

Ivey, A., & Authier, J. (1978). *Microcounseling.* Springfield, IL: Charles C. Thomas.

Ivey, A., & Hinkle, J. (1970). *The transactional classroom.* Unpublished paper, University of Massachusetts, Amherst, MA.

Klerman, G. (1986). *Suicide and depression among adolescents and young adults.* Washington, DC: American Psychiatric Press.

Kübler-Ross, E. (1975). *Death: The final stage of growth.* Englewood Cliffs, NJ: Prentice Hall.

Kübler-Ross, E. (1969). *On death and dying.* New York, NY: Macmillan Publishing.

Miller, M. (1989). *Suicide: The preventable death.* San Diego, CA: The Information Center.

Myrick, R.D., & Bowman, R.P. (1981). *Becoming a friendly helper: A handbook for student facilitators.* Minneapolis,

MN: Educational Media Corporation.

Myrick, R.D., & Erney, T. (2000). *Caring and sharing: Becoming a peer facilitator,* (2nd ed.). Minneapolis, MN: Educational Media Corporation.

Myrick, R.D., & Sorenson, D.L. (1997). *Peer helping: A practical guide,* (2nd ed.). Minneapolis, MN: Educational Media Corporation.

Painter, C. (1993). *Workshop winners: Developing creative and dynamic workshops.* Minneapolis, MN: Educational Media Corporation.

Selye, H. (1974) *Stress without distress.* New York: J.R. Lippincott.

Sharpe, R. ,& Lewis, D. (1977). *Thrive on stress: How to make it work to your advantage.* New York: Warner Books.

Sorenson, D.L. (1994). *Conflict management training activities.* Minneapolis, MN: Educational Media Corporation.

Sorenson, D.L. (1992). *Conflict resolution and mediation for peer helpers.* Minneapolis, MN: Educational Media Corporation.

Sorenson, D.L., & Nord, D.A. (2002). *Discussion-provoking scripts for teens.* Minneapolis, MN: Educational Media Corporation.

Steiner, C. (1977). *The original warm fuzzy tale.* Rolling Hills Estate, CA: Jalmar Press.

Tubesing, N., & Tubesing, D. (Eds.) (1983). *Structured exercises in stress management: Volume I.* Duluth, MN: Whole Person Press.

Varenhorst, B. (1983) *Real friends: Becoming the friend you'd like to have.* San Francisco, CA: Harper & Row.

Warshaw, R. (1994). *I never called it rape.* New York: HarperPerennial.

Wegscheider, S. (1981). *Another chance: Hope and health for the alcoholic family.* Palo Alto, CA: Science and Behavior Books.

Wiehe, V., & Richards, A. (1995). *Intimate betrayal: Understanding and responding to the trauma of acquaintance rape.* Thousand Oaks, CA: Sage.